William Augustus Miles, King of Great Britain George IV

A letter to the Prince of Wales

on a second application to Parliament to discharge debts wantonly

contracted since May, 1787

William Augustus Miles, King of Great Britain George IV

A letter to the Prince of Wales
on a second application to Parliament to discharge debts wantonly contracted since May, 1787

ISBN/EAN: 9783744740609

Printed in Europe, USA, Canada, Australia, Japan

Cover: Foto ©ninafisch / pixelio.de

More available books at **www.hansebooks.com**

TENTH EDITION.

A

LETTER

TO THE

PRINCE OF WALES,

&c. &c.

Price Two Shillings.

A

LETTER

TO THE

PRINCE OF WALES,

ON

A SECOND APPLICATION

TO

PARLIAMENT,

To discharge Debts wantonly *contracted since May,* 1787.

" His Majesty could not however expect or desire the assistance of this House, but on a well-grounded expectation, that the Prince will avoid contracting any debts in future, and his Majesty has the satisfaction to observe, that the Prince has given the fullest assurance of HIS determination to confine his future expences WITHIN his income, and had settled a plan, and fixed an order in those expences, which it was trusted, would effectually secure the execution of his intentions "

King's Message delivered to the House of Commons, May, 1787.

THE TENTH EDITION ENLARGED;

TO WHICH IS ADDED

A NEW POSTSCRIPT.

London:

PRINTED FOR J. OWEN, NO. 168, PICCADILLY, FACING BOND-STREET.

PREFACE

TO THE

TENTH EDITION.

THE rapidity with which the former editions of this Letter have been fold, demonftrates that the country, indignant at the little regard fhewn by the Prince of Wales to the diftrefs of the times, and to the fanctity of his own engagements, refents with becoming warmth, a conduct as impolitic, as it is univerfally felt and acknowledged to be fhameful and iniquitous.

The queftion agitated in the Houfe of Commons on the 14th of May, was of the utmoft importance to the internal quiet of the empire, and may ultimately affect the life, property and perfonal liberty of every individual in the Britifh dominions; the iffue which it has had, tends to favor the fanguinary views of thofe who wifh to convert our night-cellars into revolutionary tribunals, and to erect guillotines in all our public fquares. Even the interefts of pofterity are involved in this unfortunate, this more than injudicious queftion, and the gentlemen who have contended for the payment of debts which the nation has certainly no right to difcharge, and which it ought not to have known, would have done much better by reflecting, that fuch a meafure would give irrefiftible force to the arguments of thofe who object to the *expence*, and deny the *utility* of Monarchy; they fhould have well confidered the juftice of the application, the *expediency* of acceding to it, and above all, whether from the temper of the times, and the perilous ftate of the country, the very credit and exiftence of Parliament might not be endangered by complying with what was evidently its duty to have peremptorily rejected. It may not have occurred to them perhaps, that, by even condefcending to *difcufs* the fubject of the Prince's debts, they have juftified the clamor of thofe who are the moft violent in favor of democracy, while by admitting that thofe debts *ought* to be difcharged, they have proved themfelves to be very unthrifty, if not very unfaithful ftewards of the public money. The queftion well analyfed, and reduced to plain matter of fact, was, whether the Prince of Wales fhall be allowed to impoverifh and difhonor the country by profufion and bad example; whether he shall be permitted to lavish, with or without control, the property of others; Or, whether the Commons of Great Britain, faithful to themselves and to their constituents, would discharge the trust repoſed in them like BRITONS, and spurn a request which, stript of the forms prescribed by the constitution, is neither more, nor leſs than a DEMAND, and a demand of such a nature, as to leave no doubt, in even the most sceptical mind, what we have to expect from the justice and generosity of his Royal Highneſs, were we unhappily left at the mercy of either! It is our boaſt, and certainly our felicity, that we have *other* and *better* securities.--Pray heaven it may never be neceſſary to recur to them!---The report that Mr. Fox and Mr. Sheridan intended to vote for the payment of debts, contracted in direct violation of a solemn and positive engagement to Parliament, appears to have been nearer allied to truth than is consistent with the obligations which these gentlemen voluntarily impoſed upon themselves, and which they stand pledged to perform, if their repeated declarations to the different popular societies, to which they have paid ſervile and unremitting court, were ever meant to be realised. The sincerity of their attachment to the cause of the people, which has long been questioned, is now no longer doubtful. Their conduct on the 14th of last May has decided a controversy no otherwise interesting to the nation, than from the very little portion of good faith and public virtue, which unhappily exist in the country. The opportunity was certainly favorable to the recovery of their faded reputation, if the rectitude and vigor of their minds had been equal to the effort; but they were apprehensive, perhaps, of appearing, not in the engaging and amiable light of wise and faithful counsellors to his Royal Highness, but as accomplices in the shameful prodigality which has degraded him in the opinion of those, who would much rather have cause to adore, than to execrate him, and who are grieved to behold him brought forward, not in the exalted and enviable character of heir apparent to the British diadem, not as a Prince entitled to esteem, reverence, and affection, but as a mendicant, to relieve whose necessities, our pockets are reluctantly and disdainfully opened! The House of Com-

unprecedented as it is unmerited; but has the nation concurred in the vote?----No! The general voice is decidedly againſt it, and the advocates for parliamentary reform contend more forcibly than ever, for the neceſſity of cleanſing the Augean ſtable, before its accumulated and peſtilential filth, contaminates and poiſons the whole atmoſphere!--No wonder that one of the gentlemen, who has partaken of the profuſion at Carleton Houſe, kept aloof from the danger that menaced his popularity; his patriotiſm (lame and defective) halted on the day of trial, between the heir apparent and the people; for the gentleman has *courted* both, and having *pledged* himſelf to both, would no doubt have been happy with *either dear charmer,*

> But as they thus teazed him together,
> To neither a word would he ſay.

His friend and patron, more manly and correct in ſentiment and in conduct, faced the danger, and deprecated the diſcuſſion of a queſtion ſo diſreputable to the Prince, and hazardous in its conſequences to the nation. How far the gentlemen above mentioned are implicated in the guilt and profuſion of Carleton Houſe is needleſs to inquire.---Their sun, I hope, is set for ever!---and though I am disposed to treat with silent contempt the suspicious, not to say perfidious absense of one of them from his duty in parliament, I cannot but admire the happy dexterity of the other, who, in paying court at the same time, to his Royal Highness and the people, worshipped at once both God and Mammon! Instead of that eloquence which has so often cozened our judgment, and ravished our deluded senses, being exerted with all its force and ingenuity to rescue the treasury from premeditated rapine; instead of its being displayed in all its bewitching splendor, to illumine, convert and captivate a shameless senate to a sense of honor and of duty; instead of its majestic thunder, provoked by outrage, and aggravated by audacity, reverberating from one extremity of the empire to the other; instead of reprobating, as heretofore, with all the vehemence of a mind ardent in its pursuits, and in love with right, a wanton expenditure of the public money, or any addition to the aggravated burthens which oppress and discourage industry, we find its vigor, brilliancy, candor, and apparent rectitude, exchanged for insipidity, dulness, fallacy, and evasion; while the wretched effects of a vicious education, confirmed by long habits, and which interest and ambition (under the deceitful veil of mock-patriotism) had for some time past concealed from vulgar observation, appeared in all their genuine baseness and deformity! Never did the House of Commons (accustomed and reconciled as it is to sophisms, tergiversations, contradictions and absurdities) hear a speech so little calculated to answer its delusive purposes; it was artful, but could not impose; instead of giving hope or satisfaction to either party, it discouraged, offended, and disgusted both. It gave us the idea of Cunning outwitting herself by the nicety of refinement, and the only part which gentlemen were disposed to condemn the least, was that which recommended a mode less tedious for discharging the debts of the Prince of Wales, than that which was suggested by the Chancellor of the Exchequer; the motive to which, perhaps, was compassion to the object of the debate, in order that the recollection of the insult and wrong offered to the nation, might be the sooner effaced from its memory. Mr. Fox, insensible to the interests of those, whose cause he would be thought to espouse; regardless of his solemn and repeated promises to his constituents; forgetful at once of his duty, his country, and himself, descends to accelerate by subterfuge, trick, and collusion, what he publicly affects to condemn! And is this a proper person to be entrusted with the administration of a great empire? Is this the man, who, with his disgraceful history strong in our recollection, aspires to direct our public councils, and on whose admission into office every department in the State would be inundated with a croud of hungry and rapacious expectants, besides an innumerable swarm of Treasury, Admiralty, and Bedchamber Lords, assembled and embossed together, like bees impatient to hive; and in whose exclusion the nation is interested on the score of œconomy alone, independant of a variety of other considerations, no less obvious and important.

Mr. Fox tells us, in excuse for assenting to the proposed increase, that he was an advocate, when in office, for the enormous addition proposed to be made to an establishment, which every dispassionate man, acquainted with the origin and true principles of government, will acknowledge to be a very competent, and even a very liberal provision for the eldeft fon of the chief magiftrate. Mr. Fox, aware of the danger of being thought a partifan of the Prince, or of contending that the nation ought to pay his debts, enters into an hiftorical detail of his own munificent intentions towards his Royal Highnefs, at thofe precife periods of his life, when he appears to have been the leaft entitled to the liberality of the country, and the leaft difpofed to have made a proper ufe of it.

I am unwilling to fuppofe, that he antedates his beneficent intentions towards the Prince, in order to avoid an inveftigation of what might ultimately affect his own credit, and at all events degrade his Royal Highnefs ftill lower, if poffible, in the public opinion; I fhould be forry to queftion the veracity of a man, whofe talents and attainments I have been accuftomed from my infancy to admire; whofe fplendid abilities qualify him for the firft offices in the ftate, and whofe amiable and engaging manners, render his acquaintance a defirable acquifition; I would not have it thought that I affume a fact for the malevolent purpofe of drawing conclufions unfavorable to his character; but, allowing that his assent to the enormous establishment proposed by Mr. Pitt, was *not* an expedient to provide for this shameful accumulation of debt; admitting that his proposal to compel the Prince to live upon a reduced income, until that debt was liquidated, was not an artifice to impose upon our credulity, and preserve to himself, if possible, all that remains of a popularity as laboriously acquired, as it appears to have been foolishly squandered, what does it prove, but that Mr. Fox, at variance with himself, and regardless of that œconomy which he recommends to those whom he has endeavoured to supplant, would long since have plunged the nation into expences it can ill afford, and have saddled it with an establishment unnecessarily extravagant? To every objection that was made in the debate, and to a painful enumeration of facts, at once offensive and distressing, he gave no other answer, than " *that it was requisite to support the splendor of the heir apparent.*" I do not like vague terms in argument, and especially when the subject requires precision. Mr. Fox is a man of observation and of reflection; and as his mind is naturally inquisitive and acute, it cannot have efcaped his notice, that example, in fafhion and in morals, defcend from the higher to the lower orders in fociety. Mr. Fox cannot have travelled thus far on his journey through life, without having acquired a very competent knowledge of the reciprocal duties, and relative conditions of men living together in fociety; taking it then for granted, that his well-informed mind can receive no additional inftruction on a fubject, which muft have occupied a confiderable fhare of his attention, I will afk him if he does not think, that the fplendor of princes is beft fupported, not by a piebald affemblage of ufelefs valets, decorated with titles or with liveries, but by the rectitude of their conduct, and the purity of their manners? I am fure that he muft agree with me. Would to heaven that I could return the compliment, and fubfcribe with equal juftice to *his* opinions. But he has objects in view far different to thofe of mine, or he would never have afked in the face of parliament and the world, " *If they would have the Prince of Wales fet the firft example of reform?*" The very queftion is an acknowledgment of either guilt or folly, or both, in his Royal Highnefs, and the fact admitted, I anfwer in the AFFIRMATIVE. This gentleman, in a fpeech which reflects more credit on his ingenuity than on his patriotifm, afferts, *" that the cities of London and Weftminfter, and even the nation at large, fhould fet an example of reform; and that until they fhew a difpofition in earneft to retrench their expenfive habits, it is neither fair nor decent to expect temperance or œconomy in his Royal Highnefs!"* This is granting a long furlough indeed to folly and extravagance, and with which, every blockhead and knave in the kingdom will be delighted; but is it juft? and can it be faid to come with propriety from the lips of a man who is a legiflator? who has formerly filled one of the firft departments in the ftate, and who (reduced to mendicity by the irregularities of a long protracted youth) is at this inftant maintained by fubfcription! That Mr. Fox fhould have hazarded fuch fentiments, and have held fuch language, muft be matter of aftonifhment to thofe who have heard him reafon on other fubjects, and his friends I am fure muft lament, that he fhould have loft an opportunity fo favorable to the recovery of his bankrupt reputation; they muft have been hurt, that a man from whom better principles and better arguments are expected, should have offered an apology so extremely futile, and as profligate as it is weak, for the unpardonable excesses of Carleton House; they must have blushed at the humiliating and disgusting inequalities which appeared in a mind fitted for better purposes, while the miserable shifts to which Vice and Indiscretion were driven, in attempting to conceal their deformities, gave Virtue the triumph she deserves, and atoned in some degree for the indignity offered to morals and good sense. Does Mr. Fox speak of London in its corporate capacity, or as a town, containing an innumerable crowd of inhabitants promiscuously assembled together, who have a right to exact, or at least to expect, conformity to their modes, manners, and principles from their sovereign, and the male branches of his family, to whom only I have alluded, and in whom amendment is required? Never was an evasion so grosly impudent and palpable, presented to the common sense of mankind! Called upon in his public function to condemn, what in his private character he has countenanced and connived at, no wonder that the gentleman should appear aukward and ill at ease; his situation was distressing, and feeling for the wounded honor of the Prince, it was natural that he should feel for his own.

But aukward and ill at ease as he must necessarily have felt, distressed as he must have been by the vote he was called upon to give, and which, to whatever side it leant, would tend equally to his shame and conviction, I am astonished at his daring to inquire if *gentlemen would select his Royal Highness for the first example of reform, and, in some sort, for punishment?* (*a*) Yes! most undoubtedly his Royal Highness ought to be selected *for the first example of reform, and in some sort for punishment,* because he set a bad example when it was incumbent on him, as heir apparent, to have set a good one. It is a sorry and a contemptible excuse, unworthy of his pride and understanding, to say that the times are corrupt. They are indeed most lamentably so; but I will take upon me to assert, that however *bad* the morals of the country were, when his Royal Highness descended from the nursery, that he has contributed to

---

(*a*) Vide the speech of Mr. Fox, as reported in the Morning Chronicle on Friday, May 15, 1795.

make them *worfe*. The fhare he has had in relaxing thofe ligaments which unite and bind men together, and which are the eafieft, and to a certainty the beft fecurities for their mutual integrity towards each other, requires that his Royal Highnefs fhould be the firft to fet an example of reform; and if, by exercifing the virtue of felf-denial, Mr. Fox means *punifhment*, I aver that every retrenchment the Prince fhall think proper to make, will tend to reftore to him that fhare in our affections, which he has unhappily loft by mifconduct. It will be an *amende honorable*; the only one in his power to make, and which he owes to the nation whofe property he has fquandered, and whofe morals he has infulted. To thefe confiderations, which a life of thoughtlefs diffipation has rendered perfonally applicable to the Prince, may be added others not lefs obvious and important; and thefe are the obligations he is under from his elevated ftation, to fet a good example to the nation, and to abftain from whatever tends to propagate vice and immorality. It was the duty of thofe with whom he affociated in earlier life, to have informed him that the inferior orders of mankind take their morals and manners from their superiors, and that the example of the former never influence the conduct of the latter.

When the indecency of contracting debts in breach of a solemn promise was urged, when the nature and complexion of those debts, and the impertinence of calling upon the public to fulfil the engagements of vice and folly were commented upon, Mr. Fox observed a profound silence; there was nothing to revolt or shock his feelings in the turpitude that involved his Royal Highness in difficulties; there was nothing scandalous or offensive in the violation of *that* word which ought to be held as sacred as religion! neither could Mr. Fox, watchful as a lynx over all the other disbursements of public money, discover either prodigality, mischief, or breach of trust to the nation, in voting a considerable portion of its property to discharge the debts of a man who must blush, if he has any shame, to the last moment of his existence at having contracted them. Mr. Fox gets rid of the complicated infamy of the business, by asserting that he was, when in office, for allowing his Royal Highness an annual income of one hundred and twenty-five thousand pounds, but that he was over-ruled in the cabinet.

What is this, but a positive and direct confession, that his colleagues, more faithful to the nation than himself, were better guardians of the public money? What is it in fact, but acknowledging that Mr. Pitt, more frugal and œconomical, is the better minister? that he has saved to the country by his arrangement, something more than half a million; while Mr. Fox, if *his* counsels had been attended to, at a time when the heir apparent certainly "*did not differ in political opinions from his Majesty's Ministers,*" would have lavished upwards of seven hundred thousand pounds of the public money on a prodigal, whose present embarrassments would not have been prevented, either by the servile complaisance of the minister, or the bounty of the nation? This saving, immense as it is, may however be the least part of the obligations which we owe to the colleagues of Mr. Fox in the first instance, and to the prudent management of Mr. Pitt in the second. Our obligations to both may go to an extent which sets calculation at defiance, if we seriously contemplate the mischiefs which might have resulted to the kingdom, if Carleton House, at the time

---

* Vide the speech of Mr. Fox on the 14th, or 18th of May.

of the Regency, had poſſeſſed the means of addreſſing itſelf more effectually to the venal and neceſſitous, who are known to vote on the ſame principle, that the Swiſs fight, and who are to be bought and ſold like ſheep in Smithfield market. If the partiſans of the Prince ſhould imprudently urge the diſcuſſion, which every friend to the conſtitution moſt ſincerely wiſhes had never been agitated, it may not be uſeleſs to inquire how much of the preſent debt was contracted at that lamentable period, for the purpoſe of rewarding the mean and perfidious apoſtacy of thoſe, who deſerted their ſovereign in the moment of affliction. No doubt but both theſe deſcriptions of men have had a conſiderable portion of the ſpoil; and we know to a certainty, that the editor and proprietor of the Morning Poſt inſiſted on ample ſecurity, for the punctual payment of the money and annuity for which the paper was ſold, before he would transfer his ſhare in a proſtitute print to his royal ſucceſſor. I do not wiſh to bear hard upon the gentlemen, whoſe counſels at that period, are ſaid to have influenced his Royal Highneſs. It is very probable that a too rigid ſcrutiny into the tranſactions of thoſe days, would lead to a discovery not much to their honor; and apprehensive of this danger, they have preferred risking that credit with the nation to which they aspire, to an exposure of facts which would prove how very much their *principles* and their *professions* are at variance; that having had a share in the dissipations of the Prince, it is incumbent on them to extricate his Royal Highness from difficulties in which they have contributed to involve him, and that, accomplices in the guilt and folly which have excited a ferment throughout the nation, they are bound to vote for the discharge of a debt, every item of which is a disgrace to the moral character of the man who contracted it. Admitting these facts, for I am not inclined to dispute them, and allowing that for the sake of consistency, blended perhaps with a wish to partake again of the festivities at Carleton House, they cannot abandon the Prince in his greatest need, I have only to hope that neither of them in future will have the impertinence to boast of their patriotism and public virtue, or to claim the confidence of the people, whose credulity they have abused, and whose interests they seem willing to sacrifice.

THE

PUBLISHER

TO THE

READER.

London, May 14, 1795.

THE following pages were sent by the post to the publisher, accompanied by a request that he would instantly get them printed. On receiving this requisition, he resolved to relinquish the design he had formed of reprinting some letters addressed to the Prince of Wales in 1784, under the signature of Neptune, and which were at that time extremely popular; but finding, on a re-perusal, that they contained matter well worthy of the attention of his Royal Highness, and which (by omitting some circumstances applicable to the politics of the day) might be acceptable to those, who estimate the importance of Princes, not by their titles, but their virtues; and who reverence men for their good qualities, rather than for their rank or good fortune; the publisher has, in some degree, pursued his original plan, by annexing the letters in question, (reduced into one) to the following address, with a view to rescue the country from the extortion of those from whom better conduct is expected, and whose example must have a very considerable influence on the morals and manners of the nation. If the Prince of Wales should take offence at the exposure of what has long ceased to be classed among the *indiscretions* of youth; it is neither to the Author nor to the Publisher of this Address, that his Royal Highness should direct his anger, but to HIMSELF, and to those who have so scandalously misled him. He has repeatedly been admonished, in public and in private, of the sad and disgraceful consequences which would inevitably result from a life of riot and dissipation. Nor was the respect due to his own exalted character omitted, when he was apprised of the obligations which he owes to the country at large. The Letter signed Legion, annexed to that of Neptune, records a transaction which, disreputable as it is, would most probably have been effaced from our memory, if any thing like reform or contrition had appeared in the party to whom it relates, or if he had shewn even the most distant regard for the interests of his country; but, unfortunately, the contrary is the fact;

and circumſtanced as the nation unhappily is at this awful, at this tremendous criſis, me‑naced with civil broil, and engaged in a pe‑rilous war, it is become more than ever ex‑pedient, that the *prodigality* of Princes ſhould be, as their power has been---reſtrained, within the limits of Sobriety and Reaſon.

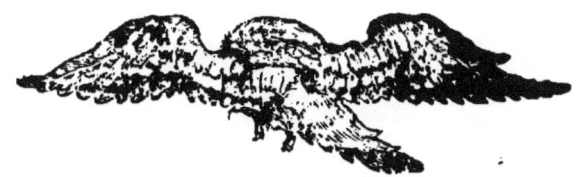

TO THE
PRINCE OF WALES,

&c. &c. &c.

May 11, 1795.

SIR,

It is sincerely to be lamented, that amidst the various descriptions of people with whom your Royal Highness has associated, none of them have had the virtue to impress upon your mind the necessity of confirming the assurance given by His Majesty in 1787, that *you would avoid contracting any debts in future*; and it is no less to be regretted, that the force and importance of the truth contained in the speech prefixed to this letter, was never suggested to you, by those whose personal interests alone required, that the strictest rectitude and propriety should mark every action of your life. The familiarities to which most of them have been admitted, and the confidence with which many of them have been indulged, would have authorised an admonition so deserving of your attention, and so intimately connected with your honor and happiness. Duty, as well as friendship, would have justified the freedom of such salutary advice, and a very trifling attention on your part, would have preserved you from the disgraceful humiliation of having publicly received it, in the severe and poignant language of well merited reproof. Unhappily for the credit of your own reputation, and no less so for the country which maintains you in splendor, many of those, whom it was your misfortune to select for companions, imagined they had an interest in deceiving you; while others, vain, abject and profligate, courted your favor by flattering your follies, and administering to your irregularities! I will venture to assert, Sir, that there is only *one* opinion throughout the British Empire, not only with respect to the general tenor of your conduct and the injustice of the claim, which has been injudiciously, not to say indecently made, on the abused generosity of the nation; but with regard to the *principles* and *sentiments* from which *that* conduct has unfortunately resulted. This opinion, Sir, however it may offend you, has been publicly announced to the world, not through the questionable medium of our public prints; not by the idle and loose conversations of interested individuals, influenced by private pique; nor by the disaffected few, who, enemies to Royalty, behold with malignant joy those improvident actions of yourself and family, which have a direct tendency to bring Monarchy into hazard and contempt, and from which more danger to our civil establishments is to be apprehended, than from all the inflammatory writings of all the incendiaries with which the French revolution has deluged Europe, but——BY THE COMMONS OF GREAT BRITAIN IN PARLIAMENT ASSEMBLED! It is the British House of Commons, Sir, (the most valuable and most important branch of *our* legislature) that, by unanimously hesitating (without a full attendance of its Members) to discharge debts, for which it is almost to be wished you were personally responsible, has tacitly acknowledged you are unworthy of the farther liberality of your country. If the call of the House so judiciously insisted upon by Colonel Stanley, and so prudently acceded to by the Minister, should be considered as a personal disrespect; if your pride should be offended at the check it has happily received from the demur to a request, at once unreasonable and ill-timed, it may be proper to inquire what right you had to expect a compliance, after a conduct so indiscreet (to speak with extreme tenderness of it,) and which has been so obviously incompatible with every obligation that you owe to yourself and the nation? If you imagine, Sir, that the accident of your birth conferred on you the right to squander, in every species of licentious dissipation, the revenues of the country; if you think yourself entitled, from your exalted rank, to levy contributions on our wealth and industry, and to render Parliament the mean and servile instrument of your exactions, it is full time that your Royal Highness should be undeceived with respect to the equity of your pretensions, and the extent of your power. It is full time that you should know how very much your fortune and your happiness depend upon a correct and temperate conduct, and that it was owing to the scandalous waste, profligacy and profusion of the Court of Versailles, and of its worthless Princes, that the former has been deservedly annihilated, and the latter become despicable, and degraded mendicants; harrassed and driven from state to state, pennyless, friendless, and despised, without the most distant prospect of ever regaining either a comfortable or a permanent establishment. A very few years are elapsed since these men lived in a style of splendor and magnificence, unknown to the more temperate manners of this country. Every knee became flexible at their approach, and the ready homage they received from millions, was more the spontaneous tribute of generous affection, than the servile adulation of an enslaved multitude: contrast their former glory, with their present forlorn and wretched condition! Examine the history of their profligate, spendthrift lives, and tremble as the consequences! Behold their persons proscribed by common consent, through the vast extent of territory in which they were once idolized; their claims to distinction treated with laughter and derision; their affluence exchanged for beggary; the acclamations of joy with which they were every where saluted, converted into the most poignant reproaches; and their birth, titles, and rank, treated with mockery and contempt: which ever way they turn, disgrace and infamy stare them in the face! they have not even the miserable consolation of being pitied, and if any thing can possibly add to the accumulated calamities, under which these wretched outcasts wander from place to place, it is that the better part of mankind approves of the punishment they have received for their aggravated guilt, folly and depravity. Their history, Sir, should serve as a MIRROR to Kings and Princes: *These* may behold in the conduct of the former, the destiny they may expect by following so ruinous an example. It is from the adversities of others, as well as from our own, that the most instructive lessons for our conduct in life are derived; and whatever tends to convince mankind of the *instability* of fortune, deserves their most serious attention. The sad reverse which the French Princes have experienced, ought not to be an unprofitable lesson to your Royal Highness, and forgive me, Sir, if I add, that the people, on whom you have so unreasonably called a *second* time to discharge engagements, which duty, as well as honor and gratitude, forbade you to contract, have an interest much greater than you suspect, that the example of France should be a warning to you and your family—Is it not a reproach, I will not say to your justice, but to your prudence, that you should again call on the bounty of the nation to administer to your extravagance, in the very midst of an arduous and perilous war, avowedly undertaken to secure that Conſtitution, on the preſervation of which you are dependent for food and raiment? Is it not as lamentable, as it is unaccountable, that with the very terrible example before you in a neighbouring nation, you ſhould have pertinaciouſly, nay criminally, adhered to the ſame ſyſtem of diſorderly and unjuſtifiable expenſe, which contributed to ſhake, and finally to ſubvert the throne of Louis XVIth? Is it decent, nay, Sir, is it HONEST in you to expect, for the mere gratification of your vanity, that any addition ſhould be made to the accumulated burdens of the country at the very inſtant that the genius of finance, exhauſted and diſpirited, is compelled to accept of private donations from corporate bodies, and even from individuals of all ranks, to carry on a conteſt, the great object of which is to preſerve you and your family from ruin? Is it not a reproach to your feelings Sir, that you are ſoliciting an enormous ſum from Parliament, amounting to near a million, to diſcharge debts wantonly contracted, and for which not even the ſhadow of an excuſe can be urged; while every nobleman and gentleman in the Britiſh dominions, while tradeſmen, mechanics, and manufacturers, while even the laborious poor have relinquiſhed a portion of their ſcanty pittance, and all of them have generouſly contributed to the the very extent of their means, to the defence of their country?

Will it, can it be believed by poſterity, that while all ranks and deſcriptions of men, vying with each other in a laudable zeal for the common cauſe, ſacrificed the comforts of life, and a part of their property; while munificent ſubſcriptions were cheerfully opened in every county, town, village and hamlet in the kingdom, to enable the miniſter to proſecute the war with vigor and effect, or to alleviate the calamities of thoſe who became victims to it, that the Royal Family of England *alone* ſhould have remained inſenſible to the calls of humanity and of patriotiſm, **and that** one of them in particular, uninfluenced by so many animating examples of public virtue, should require a portion of the money raised for the exigences of the state to be appropriated (not for the fair and honest purposes of his dignified establishment, but) to discharge a variety of engagements which he dares not reveal, and which parliament is bound in justice and in policy to resist? Is it not strange, Sir, that your name does not appear in any one of the public subscriptions to which the perilous conflict in which we are involved, or the unexampled distress of the times has given birth? We are told, that the laudable institution for the relief of the widows and children of our gallant seamen and soldiers is under your patronage; as if a charity of that nature and extent stood in need of any patronage but that of the public! There is indeed to every advertisement that appears from the society a vain and servile display of your name, unworthy of the committee, and of the gentleman who first proposed the institution, while the barren privilege of affixing a name no longer respectable is the sum total of your contribution! Surely, Sir, you must strangely have misconceived your relative situation with the people, as well as the generally received maxims of right and expediency, or you would never have come forward with a claim as impudent as it is hazardous and unjust, and which, with all the circumstances annexed to it, looks as if you considered the wealth and industry of the nation as your property, and that we held the honest fruits of our labour, or the more ample possessions of inheritance, not in fee, but as *stewards in trust* for your sole profit and use. It is time, Sir, that you should be recalled from the errors of your education, and of bad habits; it is time that you should be awakened from the delusion, in which it is impossible you can continue, without inevitable ruin to yourself, and mischief to the nation; every individual is interested in the success of this forcible appeal to your rectitude and discretion, and if you are wise, you will prove by the regularity of your future conduct, that the appeal has been made to a man worthy of the situation into which the accident of birth has thrown him——In May, 1787, a message from the King was delivered to Parliament, on the subject of your debts, amounting to ONE HUNDRED and NINETY-THREE THOUSANDS, SIX HUNDRED and FORTY-EIGHT POUNDS. The sum was considered as enormous, and the people as little satisfied with the part you had taken in politics as with your transactions in private life, expressed their disapprobation of your conduct in terms, which would have suggested to any well-constructed mind, the inestimable value of reputation. Your youth and inexperience were however urged in your behalf, and that unsuspecting generosity which marks the British character, induced the legislature to confide in the solemn assurance given by Majesty itself, *that your Royal Highness would avoid contracting any debts in future.* The sum of ONE HUNDRED AND EIGHTY-ONE THOUSAND POUNDS were voted, which, with the retrenchments *promised* and *expected*, was thought would effectually release you from your present, and preserve you from all future embarrassments.—I shall not be reproached, Sir, with presumption, when I assert that no authority, however respectable, should operate against *matter of fact*. I will even go farther, and maintain, that it ceases to be respectable, the instant it endeavours to evade truth, or to promote falsehood.

Your Royal Father, in 1787, stood pledged to the nation (of whose loyalty, affection, and liberality he has received abundant proofs) that you would not again trespass on its bounty; yet in April 1795—in less than eight years, His Majesty (in violation of his royal word,) comes forward with a piteous tale of woe, and folicits the country (labouring under the preffure of accumulated burdens, and engaged in a contest of the most serious nature) for a sum very little short of a million, to discharge a fresh catalogue of debts which, it was promifed, *fhould never be contracted!*

I pafs over the *pretended* fale of horfes, at the former epoch, and a variety of other indecent practices, which announced as little *delicacy* as *integrity*, in thofe who *counfelled* fuch mean and difhonorable expedients. I have not the leaft objection, that the fcandalous hiftories attached to Newmarket, and all the little contrivances to abufe the credulous fimplicity of the Nation, fhould be buried in oblivion. The times have moft woefully demonftrated, that *Princes* as well as *Plebians*, may ftand in need of an *Act of Grace*, and my juftice is not of that inexorable nature, as to infift on the full meafure of puniment, even to the greateft delinquents.——*This act of Grace* you have received, and I am willing to allow that your claim to an indulgence moft fhamefully abufed, was very admiffible at the time. Yet with every difpofition to pafs over the tranfactions of that period, I cannot excufe your fubfequent conduct.——I believe that if better maxims had been inftilled into you by thofe who had the charge of your education, or if you had been taught in later life to form a juft eftimate of the obligations you owe to fociety, that there would have been no occafion for this addrefs, or for thofe fevere, but neceffary animadverfions in parliament, which have offended your pride. But your having been *ill-advifed* by fome men, and *mifled* by others, can never juftify the demand which has been made on this country for the enormous fum of SEVEN HUNDRED THOUSAND POUNDS, and which I am afraid (confiderable as it is) will fcarce pay Ten Shillings in the Pound on the fum total of your debts! I am really incompetent to guefs, what arguments, even the minifter, with his fplendid talents, can urge in excufe for a demand which in times lefs profligate and corrupt, would be called *flagitious*; his fituation is embarraffing—The dilemma to which he is reduced by the ruthlefs junction of prodigality and rapacity, is certainly diftreffing, and even your Royal Highnefs may venture to feel for his perplexities, without being fufpected of affection or refpect for the man.—It was impoffible that Mr. Pitt, could refufe to deliver the meffage refpecting your debts, (unjuft and ill-timed as it was) without a direct breach with his Sovereign, and the hazard of expofing the Country at a very critical period, to the danger of *another* inter-regnum! while on the other hand, by complying with the commands of his Majefty, he was certain of obtaining a portion of that odium which certainly belongs exclufively to yourfelf. I think too favorably of your temper and difpofition, Sir, to fuppofe, that you can receive any gratification from the very aukward predicament in which you have contrived to place the man, who incurred your difpleafure fome years fince, by refifting a claim, the admiffion of which would have endangered the empire; but if your Royal Highnefs fhould bear in vindictive remembrance, the oppofition you met with at that time from his firmnefs and fidelity; if you fhould harbour any refentment in your mind, for his manly and dignified conduct in the affair of the Regency, your revenge muft have been amply gratified, by the ungracious tafk which has been impofed on him, of applying to Parliament on your behalf for money to difcharge improvident debts, and Jew bargains, at the very inftant he could not obtain fufficient for the defence of the empire, without adding very confiderably to the innumerable taxes, by which the Nation is moft oppreffively and fhamefully burthened?—Mr. Pitt may have acted prudently, in hazarding his fame and popularity, in preference to the risk of leaving the country a *second time* without a government—The concession may have averted a calamity of much greater extent than subscribing to, or in other words, encouraging your excesses; but if he has pledged himself to support the unpalatable measure in parliament, with all the credit, influence, and authority of office, he has done more than he ought to have done, and no longer deserves to be the minister of this country. —It must be matter of sincere affliction, Sir, to every man who has a just estimate of the excellence of the British Constitution, and whose loyalty to your family is neither servile nor assumed, but rational and unaffected, that the King should have been so ill-advised as to apply to parliament to relieve you a *second time* from pecuniary difficulties, after a positive assurance in 1787, that " *he would not have desired or expected the assistance of the House of Commons, but on a well-grounded expectation that your Royal Highness would avoid contracting any debts in future.*" This declaration, Sir, ill accords with the message delivered by the Chancellor of the Exchequer on the 27th of last month, and which, from the *manner* it was received, and the *comments* it excited, must have produced very unpleasant sensations in his Majesty's breast, who, in giving way to a tenderness *ill-bestowed*, has made it a question with a very considerable part of the community, whether *he* has shewn that attention to the embarrassed situation of the country, which the people have a RIGHT to expect from their sovereign? I do not wish to add to the poignancy of his feelings on an occasion so distressing, but the measure was certainly injudicious, if not hazardous, that brought on a discussion from which no credit could possibly result to *your* character, and which *policy* should have compelled you to avoid, (at a moment like the present) when the very onerous establishment of Monarchy is invidiously contrasted with the moderate expences of a Government less complicated and splendid. It is possible, that this indiscreet anxiety in his Majesty to extricate you from difficulties, resulting from riot and extravagance, may diminish that love and veneration, which a loyal and generous nation has hitherto demonstrated for your family; nor can it be attributed to caprice or disaffection, if the marked, and scandalous indifference, which a life of dissipation evinces for the miseries of mankind, should weaken that respect for your Royal Highness, which you have been taught to consider as a *tribute* due to your birth. Is it not a reproach to your justice, as well as to your prudence, Sir, (for you are no longer an infant, neither can you plead ignorance or inexperience in excuse for your excesses) that your debts, amounting to ONE HUNDRED AND NINETY THREE THOUSAND, SIX HUNDRED AND FORTY EIGHT POUNDS *(a)* in the year 1787, and for the *discharging* of which, you received that sum from the ill-requited bounty of the nation, should have grown, in the short period of eight years, to the monstrous and unpardonable size of a MILLION?

Is it not an impeachment at once of your gratitude and understanding, Sir, to expect that the people who so cheerfully contributed to your support, and who have already subscribed most liberally to your ease, splendor, and independance, should lay themselves under additional imposts, because you have been imprudent, or *something worse?*

Is it not a reproach to your feelings, Sir, that while the middle and lower orders of society can with difficulty obtain the common necessaries of life; while the aggregate taxes which every individual pays to the exigencies of the State,

---

(a) Vide the Annual Register, 1787, page 130, for the item of the first debt. The items of the second, it is thought, will never appear.

amount to, at leaſt, ſeventeen ſhillings in the pound, and that while the laborious poor *(a)*, ſmarting under the ſevere

---

a The miſerable peaſant, deſtitute of every reſource but induſtry, to ſupport his wretched offspring, and even that reſource (poor and ſcanty as it is) a contingency on his health and capacity for labor, muſt toil hard for the ſolitary ſhilling with which he daily feeds and clothes his helpleſs family. It has repeatedly fallen within my obſervation, ſince the commencement of this letter, to behold in a variety of inſtances, this extreme diſtreſs aggravated by the illneſs or infirmity, of the children to whom, as well as to their hapleſs parents, exiſtence appears to be every thing but a bleſſing. Contraſt their deplorable condition with your own exalted ſtate! Recollect how much you are indebted to *chance* for the ſuperiority of your fortune; and remembering that theſe men are your fellow-creatures; poſſeſſing, in common with yourſelf, a right to the common neceſſaries and enjoyments of life, let me aſk you, Sir, if you can without bluſhing demand, excluſive of the very ample income allowed you by the nation, a ſum that would comfortably maintain, in perpetuity, ONE THOUSAND SEVEN HUNDRED of theſe very people whoſe afflictions you would increaſe, and whoſe morſel of bread you would embitter and render more difficult to obtain, in order to defray your extravagance? Sir, it is againſt reaſon; it is againſt juſtice, humanity, and right; it is againſt your perſonal intereſt and ſecurity, that a diſproportion ſo ſcandalous and unnatural ſhould exiſt between MAN and MAN! God never deſigned it; and the Government that authoriſes or connives at the abuſe, hazards its tranquillity or exiſtence. It is no abatement of the ſufferings and agoniſing ſorrows of the famiſhed cottager, that the portion of happineſs is no more diffuſed among the higher than it is among the lower orders of ſociety. It is no alleviation of his diſtreſs that while he is periſhing of hunger, your Royal Highneſs is expoſed to numberleſs vexations and diſappointments. The chagrin and anger, provoked by pride, deſervedly mortified, or your ill-health, ariſing from intemperance, afford him no conſolation in the hour of calamity; they adminiſter no comfort to his mind, and afford no drawback to his grief or misfortunes.

They furniſh neither food nor raiment to his ſtarving, ragged offspring, nor ſhield his ill thatched hovel from the rude blaſts of winter. It is ſophiſtry to ſay that the magnificence in which you live is but a ſplendid miſery, which amply revenges him for the difference of his fortune; nor is it argument to ſay, that becauſe you are wretched, he ought to be happy, for it is only a baſe and vindictive mind that can derive conſolation or joy from the miſeries of another!

pressure of hunger, have been forced, in order to prolong a wretched existence, into insurrection of a very serious and alarming nature; that you, insensible to their deplorable condition, and to the accumulated calamities which mark the present time, should come to Parliament, and require those burdens to be increased, and those calamities to be augmented, without producing any one voucher that could justify Parliament to the nation for so lavish a grant of the public money? Will your Royal Highness reveal the disgraceful items which have swelled your present debt to a sum, which renders your application for its payment as preposterous, as it is indecent and inconsiderate? I am sure you will not, and for the best of all possible reasons, because

YOU DARE NOT!

I will not inquire, whether the money advanced in 1787, was faithfully applied to the ostensible purposes for which it was asked and granted; neither will I inquire, whether those œconomical arrangements took place, for which you stood pledged to Parliament and your country; nor is it necessary; the message delivered to the House of Commons on the 27th of last month is a sufficient answer to every question of the kind: it is a direct and evident violation of the contract, in its most *essential* part, and enables

---

Would you wish, Sir, to have your demand prefaced by the causes that produced it? Would you hazard a proclamation that should announce to the MILLION who subscribe to your maintenance, that the splendid allowance of ONE HUNDRED THOUSAND POUNDS a year is inadequate to your support, and that the sum (ample as it is) must be doubled? I do not think, Sir, that you would consent to any such statement. Yet, whether you decline it from modesty or from fear, the injustice and indecency of taking so much money from the acquired wealth of the country, will not be less enormous; and you will do well to abandon what you cannot demand as a right, and which the most servile of your dependants will not venture to assert you are entitled to receive as a favor.

us to ascertain, with almost mathematical precision, the fidelity with which *the other conditions of the bond* have been fulfilled; but though I am willing to spare you the mortification which detected fallacy must ever feel, whether it is found in a cottage or a palace; although I forbear, from motives of affection and loyalty to your family, to enter into a scrutiny which certainly would not tend to inspire the people with a love of royalty; I feel no difficulty in asserting that, considering all the circumstances attending your present incumbrances, the *mode* in which, and the *purposes for which* they were contracted, with the positive assurauce from Majesty itself, that no future claim of the kind should ever be brought forward, that the House of Commons cannot vote for the payment of your debts without being guilty of a breach of trust, and forfeiting the confidence of the nation!

THE LETTERS OF NEPTUNE

TO THE

PRINCE OF WALES;

Occafioned by the countenance given to a fet of men who oppofed his father's government from the worft of motives, and for the worft of purpofes.

SIR, JULY, 1784.

While your irregularities were confined within the circle of juvenile indifcretions, and your conduct could be accounted for in the natural progrefs of the paffions, your exceffes, numerous as they have been, excited indeed our wonder, but never provoked our indignation. We beheld you emerge from the nurfery with even paternal affection; every heart was devoted to your intereft; and it was neither difficult nor unworthy of you to have preferved thofe prejudices which had been generoufly formed in your favor. The intemperance of your youth gave no offence; and in the commencement of your career, it was never once fufpected that we fhould have occafion to execrate the object whom we adored.

Such, Sir, were the advantages under which you entered into fociety; and give me leave to inform you, that you muft have been extremely indefatigable to have effaced fo effectually thofe favorable impreffions, and to have changed the current of opinion againft you in fo fhort a time.

To your imprudent choice of friends may be attributed your prefent painful fituation.

It was your misfortune to felect thofe for your companions, who, having neither fortune nor character to lofe, were ready to conduct you into all the extravagancies of the meanest and most dangerous debaucheries. Their profligacy rendered them the willing panders to your pleasures, while their poverty involved you in their profusion and necessities. The nation feels the consequences of these complicated evils, and beholds with equal astonishment and indignation, a progress uncommonly rapid from bad to *worse*, and which may eventually terminate in serious mischief to yourself and your country.—It must have been no less mortifying to your royal father than disgraceful to yourself, that the first public act of your life was distinguished by an indecent opposition to the measures of his Government, and the constitutional rights of his crown: it would be difficult to account for the motives of so decided and so extraordinary a conduct, if the party with whom you have condescended to associate, had not revealed the conditions of your contract. The engagements on your part have been executed with the most active and pointed fidelity, with a firmness, which has triumphed over every obligation of filial duty and respect, and rendered you insensible to the general interests of your fellow citizens. I will pass over the moral turpitude of irritating a son against a father: the infamy of the action will decidedly fall on the incendiaries, but the sad consequences resulting from a conduct so atrocious, may ultimately affect the peace and prosperity of the nation, that has a claim on your gratitude in return for the splendor and liberality with which it supports you.

To those who have abused your simplicity and inexperience, I have little to say: long habits have rendered them incorrigible, and admonitions become useless; where there is neither shame nor sentiment to give them force. Is it possible, Sir, that those who have had the important charge of your education, could have concealed from your knowledge the forms and spirit of the constitution?

It is neceffary to inform you, that before the man to whom you look up, can perform his promife, two events, not very likely to happen, muft pofitively take place; he muft be reftored to power in the firft inftance—and in the fecond, the NATION muft confent to the increafe of income with which you have been flattered and deluded.

The public, Sir, are under no obligation to difcharge thofe debts, which your profufion has created; nor is it very probable that, confidering the deplorable ftate of their finances, they will be eafily prevailed upon to enlarge an income, already fufficient for all the honeft purpofes of your prefent eftablifhment.

Thefe circumftances, perhaps, have been artfully concealed from you, as well as the impoverifhed ftate of the kingdom, which will not admit of a wanton and unneceffary expenditure of the public money. The war with America, ruinous in every refpect, idly began and more idly conducted, has oppreffed the people with innumerable taxes, and rendered them almoft incapable of fuftaining any additional burthens. Yet, the author of this unfortunate and difgraceful war, whom you have every reafon to execrate, is honored with your confidence; and equally deftitute of pride and integrity, we find him content to act a fervile and fubordinate part to the man, who has repeatedly menaced him with impeachment and the block!(*a*) The cala-

---

(*a*) Lord North was faid by this gentleman to be fo extremely infamous, that he would not truft himfelf alone in the fame room with him; Mr. Fox even pledged himfelf to the nation, that his Lordfhip fhould be impeached.—The impeachment never took place, nor was it ever attempted; the gentleman confequently either broke his promife to the nation, or he afferted a calumny for the purpofe of fupplanting the minifter.

If the former; it proves Mr. Fox is not to be depended upon; if the latter; that he is not very delicate in his choice of means to obtain his object, and in either cafe that he is a very improper perfon to be entrufted with the government of the country. If Lord North deferved to perifh on a fcaffold, how comes it that Mr. Fox did not fulfil his engagement to the public, when he came into office, and declared that, "bad as he thought matters were, he found them much worfe." And if his Lordfhip was really fo infamous that all communication with him was unfafe, unlefs in the prefence of a third perfon, what muft we think of the ftrength and rectitude

F

mities occafioned by the weak and corrupt adminiftration of his Lordfhip, will terminate only with the empire; they will be felt to the lateft period of our political exiftence. The millions fquandered in obtaining majorities in both Houfes of Parliament, will render a fyftem of the ftricteft œconomy indifpenfable: and thefe truths, too obvious to be unknwon to you, fhould at leaft have taught you to reftrain your extravagance.

The plea of youth affords you no excufe. You ftand in a different predicament from that of a private gentleman. His perfon and property are anfwerable for the debts he contracts; bankruptcy and a prifon terminate his career, and the nation feels no inconvenience from his follies—but you, Sir, have *no property*; your annual income is an annual donation which may be withdrawn or withheld, and whatever your wretched affociates may affert to the contrary, the PEOPLE OF ENGLAND will never fubmit to recompenfe thofe who injure and infult them!

It is a maxim, Sir, univerfally admitted, that the people fhould have but *one* opinion of their fovereign; and this

---

of that mind which could coalefce with his Lordfhip, after having thrown fuch a ftigma on his character? What apology can Mr. Fox offer to an infulted nation for having contributed to reinftate the man in power and in truft, whom he denounced in parliament for having abufed that power and betrayed that truft? While Lord North was an obftacle to the ambition of Mr. Fox, he was a compound of vice and imbecillity, whofe crimes and follies had brought ruin on the nation; all fubfequent minifters, under fimilar circumftances, it feems have incurred fimilar reproaches; but the inftant his Lordfhip became *convenient* to the defigns, and would be *fubfervient* to the views of the Right Hon. Gentleman, his vices and incapacity were transformed into talents and virtues; no man was more worthy, none fo proper to work the falvation of his country; and lo! his Lordfhip became a fecond time the Atlas of the ftate! All the infamy attributed to his character difappeared, and Mr. Fox, who had held his Lordfhip forth as an object of public fcorn and hatred; Mr. Fox, who had declared all communication with Lord North hazardous and difreputable, fought his confidence, and, receiving him to his bofom, avowed himfelf his friend and colleague! What is this but an impudent mockery of all public and private morality; what is it but a grofs and flagitious affront offered to the nation at large, and treating it with as little honefty as good manners? Does Mr. Fox confider us as flutes to be played upon at his pleafure, and for his profit and amufement exclufively? He has indeed " *founded us, from our loweft note to the very pitch and compafs of the gamut*;" but, though he has fretted us, wronged and infulted us, " *he fhall not play upon us.*"

maxim holds equally good when applied to the presumptive Heir to the Crown.—It would be an idle waste of time to explain to you what that opinion ought to be; those, to whom your education has been confided, cannot possibly have permitted you to advance to maturity in utter ignorance of so important a truth.

It is impossible, Sir, that you can be unacquainted with the public opinion respecting your conduct! You have learned in it, the well founded, though intemperate, resentment of the people, whose honest indignation, provoked by your complicated offences, have forced them to violate the limits of respect and decency, and hurl their sentiments in your very face.—I know that you have been taught to despise the public opinion, and that the unremitting endeavours of your little Pandemonium have been exerted to inspire you with a contempt for popular applause. Adopt the idea, and your future life will be miserable—be assured, Sir, that popularity is the best security for a Prince; it is not so fluctuating as you have been told. Private individuals have found it precarious, because it has been generously advanced to them on the credit of professions which they never intended to realise, and they have sunk into obscurity on their impostures being discovered. But this is justice, not caprice.—Professions of patriotism are unnecessary where the power exists of carrying them into immediate execution. Our opinion of your Royal Highness will ever be regulated by your conduct. Deserve well, and you will never have occasion to reproach the multutude with inconstancy, or want of affection. Unhappily, Sir, the bias of your education has given way to bad example.

To fall into the hands of pimps, gamblers, and prostitutes, is among the common accidents to which every young man is exposed on his entering into society, and may be easily corrected: but you, Sir, disdaining the progressive stages to dishonor, started from the nursery into public life the very prop and hero of faction, and attached yourself to men of ruined fortunes and characters, who, under the sanction of your countenance, have attempted to annihilate at once the prerogative of the Crown and the rights of their fellow citizens.

You have, however, had the mortification to find that the credit of your name could not avail them. They have been driven from power with every mark of ignominy, and experience must have convinced you, that it was impossible to be connected with them without partaking of their infamy.

To war against experience is to give defeat the preference to conquest, and to hold honor and happiness at defiance. Believe me, Sir, the people are not to be awed by the splendor of your rank into an approbation of your errors, much less will they be disposed to support them; and you will do well to remember, that it is among the most common maxims of prudence, to avoid those contests, in which much may be lost and nothing can be gained.

If the various excesses into which you have plunged, with a precipitancy unexampled in the annals of this country, have involved you in pecuniary difficulties, you have no right to call upon the nation to extricate you.

I am very far from wishing you to be confined within the scanty limits of a penurious income; I would have it fully equal to your exalted birth and expectations; but in fixing your establishment, an attention must be paid to the finances of the nation. The former must ever depend upon the latter, and it may perhaps be matter of information to you, that every new tax, under our enormous load of debt, is an advance towards a revolution.

This is a serious and an alarming truth, which should

awaken you to a fenfe of œconomy, for the fake of yourfelf and family, fhould you have no regard for the empire to which you have an hereditary claim.

The political relation which you have to the Conftitution, gives the meaneft of your fellow citizens an intereft in your conduct. The fate of millions is involved in that of yours, and the danger to be apprehended from your conduct and long-eftablifhed habits, is fufficient to alarm even confidence itfelf. Unhappily, Sir, the people, anxious to avert the mifchiefs with which they are threatened, have in vain endeavoured to fhame you out of riot and bad company, to recal you to a fenfe of your dignity, and to the confideration of thofe tenures, by which the imperial diadem of Britain is held.

You cannot be uninformed, that the violation of them coft one Monarch his life, and another his Crown; but it may not be amifs to remind you that you are liable to the fame penalties.

When you imprudently embarked in the fervice of oppofition, it did not occur to you, perhaps, that it ought to be an invariable maxim with every branch of the Royal Family to obferve the ftricteft neutrality towards the various factions which are perpetually contending for an afcendancy in the Government; but fince your fatal and difgraceful alliance with men of the worft and moft profligate characters in the kingdom, it has been the principal object of their attention, to feduce you from the confideration of a truth, no lefs obvious than important, by plunging you into all the exceffes of expenfive riot and diffipation, as if it had been their fixt determination that your ruin fhould precede that of the empire.

Your intimacies, no lefs mean than difhonorable with fuch men, have not only excited an alarm among all ranks of people at home, but become the table-talk at every tavern and coffee-houfe on the continent, where you are more cenfured for your want of pride than for your want of prudence; and while foreigners behold with fcorn and aftonifhment the heir of Britain degrading himfelf below even the meaneft of his worthlefs companions, your fellow citizens lament, with the moft affectionate concern, your obftinate attachment to men who have neither talents, integrity, nor manners.

A momentary reflection would be fufficient to awaken you to a fenfe of your fituation: but your affociates, aware of the danger of leaving you to yourfelf, have artfully contrived to keep you in the worft of diffipations, left a lucid interval of good fenfe fhould reftore you from the delirium of pleafure to the exercife of your underftanding.

They are confcious that they muft finifh whenever you have the virtue to refume yourfelf, and they do well to keep you in profound ignorance of the dangers which furround you.

In the black catalogue of their aggravated guilt, the infamy of playing off the fon againft the father is not the leaft criminal and ingenious—it is perfectly confiftent with their principles, and favorable to their defigns, to render the former a dupe to their artifices and the latter a cypher in his dominions; but as millions are involved in your fate, it is impoffible but the clamours of the multitude will force their way through the fturdy and beggarly phalanx with which you have guarded Carleton Houfe, and counfel you to acknowledge a truth, which filial duty, independent of every political obligation, ought to have fuggefted to you.

Recollect, Sir, the hiftory of the two men who would arrogate to themfelves the firft offices of the ftate, and tremble for the confequences of your extraordinary partiality. Recollect that one of them, in time of profound peace, excited a civil war in the diftant provinces, by reviving a claim, which had been abandoned as impracticable eight years before. The colonifts, ftanding on the adamantine pillars of the Conftitution, afferted that taxation and reprefentation were infeparable. A negative was founded from the fhores of America as from the the voice of Jove; nor has the thunder of the Britifh arms been able to cancel the irrevocable fiat of truth and juftice. Fleets and armies were tranfported, at an enormous expence, to recover by violence what had been loft by folly; but as the war was as ill-conducted as it was wantonly begun, the events of the conteft were the abfolute lofs of America, a ruinous war with three great maritime powers of Europe, a diminution of commerce, revenue, and dominion, and an increafe of taxes, which puzzles the ingenuity of finance to raife even fufficient to pay the intereft of the money voted for the fupport of Government.

Is it to this wretched politician, who has deprived his country of an extent of territory equal to half of Europe, that you wifh to give your confidence? Is this blufterer in politics, whofe capacity and views extended no farther than the managememnt of his mercenaries, and who vainly thought that if he could triumph in Parliament he could triumph every where elfe—Is this great luminary, whom we now fee fallen from his fphere, and moving as one of the fatellites in the circle of an inferior planet, that once performed a fubordinate courfe round his bright orb, to be again called forth into public life, that he may complete the ruin which he began?

Is it this great minifter, degraded into a mean and fervile dependance on the very man who menaced him with the block, in the zenith of his power, for the complicated crimes of venality, treachery, and corruption, that is to work our political falvation?—Shame upon fuch folly!

Is it to such a man, Sir, that you are so anxious to confide the safety of the nation? Impossible! Were you to pronounce it in my presence, I should question the fidelity of my ears. Is it from a junction so unnatural that the most valuable appendage of the British Empire is to be preserved from following the ruinous example of America? or can you seriously believe that a pyebald ministry, composed of odds and ends and men of straw, can possibly restore this country to her former splendor? You may reckon to eternity, Sir, but all the cyphers in the universe will never make an unit.

America torn from us by the very root; Ireland on the eve of revolt, and Scotland beating the loud drum of discontent, from the Tweed to the barren Orkneys, exhibit a very gloomy and humiliating prospect; while a faction in the centre of the kingdom, under the sanction of your authority, is indefatigably employed in bringing their Sovereign and the measures of his Government into disrepute? Are you to be informed, at this period, that your very existence depends upon that of the Empire? Our acres will remain to us through every change that can possibly happen: we have only to transfer our allegiance; but a revolution consigns you to beggary and to exile. In such a moment of calamity you will not only find yourself without property, but without friends; and the vermin, who at present bask in the sun-shine of your favor, will be the first to abandon you to the rigor of your fate.

Let us however hope, that an event so melancholy to the kingdom and ruinous to yourself, will be prevented by a timely attention to the obligations, which you owe to your country, and your family.

Consider what you have at stake, and banish from your confidence and society, a set of men whose pernicious counsels and profligate manners have done equal injury to the power and the morals of the nation.

NEPTUNE.

TO THE

EDITOR

OF THE

WORLD.

On a fraudulent Transaction that happened at New-market.

SIR, Dec. 1791.

I AM as little disposed to think *ill* of a YOUNG MAN, whose interest it certainly is, that all the world should think *well* of him, as the most intimate of his bottle companions: but my opinion of him must be regulated by his *conduct*, and not by the partial or venal reports of interested individuals, to all of which, every action of his life gives a direct and positive contradiction. A recent transaction, which shrinks from investigation, and puts even impudence to the blush, has brought him forward to public notice, from the back ground into which the most wanton profusion had driven him, and that under circumstances so humiliating and disgraceful, as to extinguish every hope that compassion for his youth, and respect for his family, have hitherto entertained from the combined efforts of time and experience.

A variety of reports, on which a variety of conjectures have been formed, and a variety of random assertions made, have, for some time past, engrossed the general attention, and furnished matter for severe animadversion among all ranks and descriptions of people: but various as these reports have unavoidably been, from the circumstance that gave rise to them, being known only to a CHOSEN few, the person whose reputation only they affected, and which only could be affected by them, was the focus in which their pestilential and destructive rays finally centered. It was he ALONE who absorbed the guilt and infamy of the transaction; he alone sustains the odium; for his situation in life deprives him of the poor and sorry consolation of an associate in the crime laid to his charge. Were there ever a thousand accessaries, HE would eclipse them all—He alone would be considered as the principal, and stand alone exposed to public censure and derision!—for who, among the most necessitous and profligate of his *pretended* friends, would have presumed to suggest so foul and so iniquitous an expedient; and he that gave the advice, will he have the effrontery to avow it?

I am positive that he will not, though it were to screen the deluded youth from reproach and ignominy. The fraud was no sooner committed, than it blazed forth, in all its turpitude; Vice felt herself honoured by the audacity, as well as by the atrociousness of the trick, and gloried in what has been matter of profound grief and astonishment to every virtuous mind in the kingdom. It was at first imagined, that the splendor of rank would have dazzled the million, and afforded a shield to the dignified perpetrator: those who counted upon this security, paid but an ill compliment to the morals of the Nation. These *Gentry* have since been taught, that the morals and manners of the people are not to be violated with impunity. They have found that even the public prints, whose mistaken lenity has hitherto spared their persons and their crimes, disdained a criminal taciturnity upon the occasion, and demonstrated their patriotism by stigmatizing what they justly considered as a dishonor to the Country. Their zeal and their clamour appear to have penetrated into the very sanctorum of Turf Swindling, and to have frightened even the stoutest of the Banditti.

A mean and pitiful request was made in a succession of anonymous paragraphs, that "*the public would suspend their judgment until a certain club or combination of men, gave their report.*"—Several weeks have elapsed since the *petitions* were made; but as it was probable that the affair was too *mysterious* and *intricate* for a *prompt* decision, no objection was made to the delay. It was however expected, that these gentlemen, sitting in judgment on the character of a man so nearly related to us all, would at least *authenticate* their report by the signature of their respective names. But in this well founded hope we have been disappointed; not one of the *jurors* empanelled upon the occasion, will personally vouch for the innocence of either *master* or *man*, and to have published this extraordinary report, in the first person plural, without informing us whether it was the production of an individual or of a multitude, was an offence against grammar, as well as against sound policy, and good manners, for what confidence can we have in the verdict of an *invisible* jury? and what right has even the *first* man in this Country, to expect that we should implicitly believe an anonymous ipse dixit? instead of an explicit and ample explanation which was to establish the *innocence* of the parties, and totally to destroy every vestige of *suspicion*, a compound of impertinent and frivolous assertions and paragraphs, beginning with WE HAVE, &c. are offered to us with all the insolence of despotic authority. The story so far from being elucidated, seems, by this lame and nameless defence, to be more than ever perplexed; so far from being brought into the clear and brilliant atmosphere of truth, it seems to be more invelloped than ever, in dark and sulphurous grounds, which blacken, even to the complexion of Erebus, the hapless object whom it is pretended to bleach and purify! I can easily conceive the confusion which the necessity of doing SOMETHING in this nefarious business must have occasioned. No doubt but the distress into which so disastrous an event plunged all those who riot in Pall Mall or elsewhere, must have been considerable; no doubt but they beheld the calamity and ruin with which they were threatened by an event likely in its consequences to have produced a total and happy revolution in the sentiments of their deluded patron. The security they have long enjoyed in the public credulity, and the forbearance, added to their avowed contempt of character, made them at first indifferent to all censure, but in proportion as the buzz increased, their fears augmented, and a resolution was taken to do all that guilt could do to appear *innocent*. Affidavits sometimes impose on vulgar minds. At all events they have their convenience, when judiciously introduced, as well as an alibi, and the magistrate before whom they are sworn, by lending his name, seems to bear testimony to the truth of the assertions they contain; I do not mean to impeach the veracity of those that have been *made*, though not *produced*, on this occasion, I have every respect for the *rising* reputation, and wonderful dexterity of the groom that has been introduced to public notice with so much parade and circumstance. He may, for aught I know to the contrary, be a *gentleman* of the *strictest honor*, and most *accomplished manners*. The school in which he has been educated certainly indicates as much, and will not permit me to doubt a moment, either of his *rectitude* or *good-breeding*. Yet with all possible confidence in his *integrity* and *politeness*, and with an equal degree of reverence for the judgment of *those* who recommended this mode of exculpation, I think it was indecent, if not dangerous, to make the character of one of the most elevated men in the kingdom depend folely upon the credit which may or may not be given to the teftimony of a man in one of the very loweft, and certainly leaft honorable occupations in life, and who being unfortunately, though no doubt *undefervedly*, involved in the fame cenfure that affects his royal mafter, will find it difficult to efcape fufpicion. There may be œconomy and novelty in attempting to white-wafh *two* individuals by *one* affidavit, but I am fure there was little fkill in it. Perhaps it was an expedient of neceffity, and adopted not from any hope of its being efficacious, but merely as being the leaft exceptionable; if fo, I would afk the *pretended* friends of this haplefs youth, if even the moft virulent of his enemies (fuppofing him to have any) could poffibly degrade him to a condition more painful? Thefe remarks, however hard they may bear on the parties concerned, are not meant to preferve the unworthy fubject alive in the minds of men; on the contrary, they are meant to filence impudent and imprudent efforts to explain away what cannot be denied, and what, from my foul, I fincerely wifh had never happened. It is the fartheft from my intention to wound the feelings, or to add to the keen anguifh, which the perfon alluded to muft fuffer on finding himfelf become the tabletalk of grooms and valets. I feel for his fituation, and lament that a name which ought to be *idolized*, and a rank which ought to be *refpected*, fhould be familiarly canvaffed in the polluted mouths of the outcafts and refufe of fociety! I am amazed that his pride has not taken offence at the idea of *Vermin* fitting in judgment upon *Excellence*, and that what ought to be the boaſt and comfort of the Nation, ſhould wantonly alarm its fears and incur its reproach; I am grieved, Sir, that he ſhould be ſo inattentive to his own honor and happineſs, at a moment when the fatal conſequences ariſing from a paſſion for low and profligate company are ſo ſtrikingly evident in a branch of the Royal Family in France, and to which unfortunate propenſity may be attributed the diſaſtrous ſituation of a country, hitherto conſidered as the moſt enlightened, and moſt civilized part of the globe.

LEGION.

POSTSCRIPT.

AN attempt has been made to anfwer the preceding Letters; but if anfwers were to flow from the prefs until every type in Europe was expended, they would not be able to refute any one affertion, or to controvert any one argument contained in the foregoing pages. This is not a declaration proceeding from an arrogant and affected fuperiority over adverfaries that are forry and contemptible at the beft, but a confequence that naturally refults from having taken the *right fide* of the queftion, and from having adhered moft fcrupuloufly to *facts*, which can neither be palliated nor denied. What is matter of public notoriety cannot decently be difavowed; and if the gentlemen who, with more apparent regard to their *intereft* than to their *characters*, have attempted to apologize for dignified profligacy, had recognized the ftrong and inacceffible ground on which I have taken poft, I do not think they would have hazarded a conteft from which his Royal Highnefs is likely to receive fuch little benefit, and his champions fuch little *honor*.

It is rather unfortunate, that a pamphlet, avowedly written to fecure the Prince of Wales from what is termed "*unmerited odium*," fhould fcarce contain any thing elfe than an impeachment of the *loyalty* and *good manners* of the perfon who is faid to have attacked the heir apparent with the moſt *" unfeeling indecency."* This mode of exculpating guilt will have very little weight with thoſe who are accuſtomed to reaſon more logically, and who eſtimate the force and validity of arguments by their affinity to truth. They will, as well as myſelf, be at a loſs to conjecture, what poſſible relation there can exiſt between the vices of *one man*, and the rudeneſs of *another*; neither can it be well underſtood, why malice and diſloyalty in the latter (ſuppoſing theſe charges to be well-founded) ſhould atone for a groſs and infamous violation of every moral and political duty in the *former*.

I do not know that I learnt to make my bow from the ſame dancing-maſter that inſtructed my adverſaries, but I will venture to aſſert, that our ethics are not derived from the ſame ſource. Whether my manners have been formed on the ſyſtem recommended by the late Lord Cheſterfield, who was eſteemed the beſt-bred man of his age, or whether they reſemble thoſe of Buckhorſe, who was certainly the worſt; whether my ideas of civil government are taken from thoſe of Sir Robert Filmer, or from thoſe of Algernon Sidney, are of little import to the queſtion under conſideration; and as they do not tend to eſtabliſh either the guilt or innocence of his Royal Highneſs, they are irrelevant to the ſubject, and may poſſibly excite ſome doubts of the ſanity, as well as of the correctneſs of *that* mind which could introduce them for either purpoſe; nor is it leſs curious, that a gentleman, who has publiſhed preciſely twenty-five pages and a half of what he is pleaſed to call *Obſervations on a Letter addreſſed to the Prince of Wales*, (and which twenty-five pages, with their fraction included, are avowedly written to bleach and purify his Royal Highneſs) ſhould acknowledge much more than I have aſſerted, or even imagined. If this mode of proving the innocence of men, by establishing their guilt, could be introduced at the Old Bailey, the felons in Newgate would have little to apprehend from the verdict of a jury.

The only passages that relate to the subject in question, acknowledge the "*existence of Bacchanalian orgies* (*a*) *at Carleton House;*" that "*the Prince of Wales has kept exceeding bad company;*" that "*he ran in debt at one time to the amount of near two hundred thousand pounds;*" that "*he promised to behave better if his debts were paid; and that being paid, he broke his word, and behaved worse;*" that "*his Royal Highness came again to Parliament, for almost four times the former sum, and which sum was far more than either Sardanapalus or Heliogabalus (the worst and most infamous of mankind) could possibly have squandered in the same space of time;*" that "*the representatives of the people,*" whether wisely or honestly, is not mentioned "*thus called upon, have put these debts in a train of liquidation;*" and finally that "*not one of these debts were contracted by the man who has asked us to discharge them!*" (*b*) What is this but accusing his Royal Highness, and that

---

(*a*) Observations on the Letter addressed to the Prince of Wales, p. 7.

(*b*) A reference to the Author will best ascertain the fidelity with which I have quoted him.

"How the immense sums that have been raised have been misapplied, it is almost impossible even to guess. an transactions which would reflect such eternal disgrace upon the abettors of them, conjecture must wander wide of the mark. The public have seen debts to the amount of near *two hundred thousand pounds* contracted in a short period; they have also seen these debts discharged by parliament. It is not to be wondered, after his Majesty's message, stating a *well-grounded expectation* that the Prince would not contracting any debts in future, that his Royal Highness's *hangers-on* should en-

H

"*most unmannerly,*" *most maliciously,*" and certainly "*most disloyally,*" of obtaining money under false pretences ? what is it in fact, but pleading guilty to the indictment that has been preferred, and sueing to that tribunal to which I have appealed, for mercy on the delinquent ? If this man writes for bread, I pity him;—If to instruct us, I think he has mistaken his talents; and if to pay court to the heir apparent, I am afraid that the advantages I have derived from his testimony, will operate to his prejudice, and cancel every claim he can possibly urge to the smiles of his Royal Highness, who certainly owes very little to the judgment, whatever he may do to the zeal of such champions. If this gentleman really felt that affection which he professes for the Prince, it would have been better shewn by a profound silence on a subject which will not bear investigation, and which cannot occur to the mind, without manifest injury to his Royal Highness; the servility however of those who *out* of parliament would excuse the licentious extravagance of Carleton House, is less reprehensible than that, which would administer to it from *within*.

---

deavour to plunge him again into difficulties, because, as I have stated, and as it was generally believed, that was part of their system; but it is exceedingly to be wondered, that there should have been found in this nation, persons weak and wicked enough to trust him; or rather them, for it is impossible, if we consider the immensity of the sum, had he united the vices of Sardanapalus with those of Heliogabalus, that he could in so short a time have squandered it. However that may be, the public have seen their representatives called upon for a sum of almost four times the bulk of the former; they have seen the sum, large as it is, in a train of liquidation through the channel of parliament; they have seen men whom every one knew to have been insolvent, ever since the first of the transactions alluded to, live in a state of opulence and splendor; and when they compare these two circumstances, they will form their own opinion of this application of national propery."

Vide page 8 of the Observations on a Letter addressed to the Prince of Wales, and on those signed Neptune and Legion.

(35)

In the former inftance, its influence and example are confined within fmall limits, by the obfcurity and poverty of the parties; befides indigence has a claim to indulgence, for hunger hard preffed, may tempt a man to do that, which relieved from the preffure of famine, he would revolt at—the bafenefs cannot be very widely diffufed, and not being committed in violation of any direct and pofitive engagement, the mifchief refulting from it will be trifling and unimportant; but in the latter inftance, it affumes a more criminal and more dangerous appearance.—A PART deputed by the whole, to conduct the complicated interefts of a wide extended Empire, cannot depart from that fobriety and rectitude, to which they are pledged for the benefit of that whole; and having duties to fulfil, they fhould remember that they have a character to preferve—In them, a complaifance of the defcription which I have ftigmatifed in the former as fervility, is neither more nor lefs, than a breach of truft to the public, which the nation in general, and the immediate conftituents of the offending party in particular, are called upon to refent and punifh—A man, with a character fo foul and fo very black, that even ink cannot ftain it, feemed difpofed on the 14th of May, to have complimented his Royal Highnefs with even more than he afked; and if the favor(*a*) expected in return for this tribute of loyalty in advance, could poffibly reftore degraded reputation, the quota of the *honorable* member would be wonderfully well laid out, with a certainty of repayment and an intereft fo ufurious, that even Pulteney, or Avarice itfelf, would blufh to exact or receive it. When men of this defcription obtain feats in the Houfe of Commons, it proves that the conftituent

---

(*a*) A Peerage.

part of the nation is to the full as corrupt as their representatives, and makes the question of reform a problem much more difficult to be solved than we imagine. The man, whose proposals in parliament was treated with scorn by all parties, aims it is said at a peerage, but despairing to obtain it in the *present* reign, he assures himself to a certainty of it in the *next*, by becoming the pandar to vice. Is there any passage or sentence in either of the preceding letters that contains so severe and so pointed a satire on the principles of his Royal Highness, as the servile harangue of this worthless and litigious character? What opinion must even *this* man (who would lavish without limitation or remorse the treasures of the country on senseless dissipation) entertaid of the Prince, when he expects in return for this breach of public duty, that his Royal Highness would on his accession to the throne, select him for the British Peerage? How fallen, how very much dishonored and degraded, must the Heir Apparent appear, when the most despicable of mankind believe him capable of admitting them to his confidence and councils? I have no aversion to the hereditary nobility of England; on the contrary my respect for the aristocracy is known, and can be attested by men, whose exemplary probity, talents, and manners, justify their claim to distinction, and add lustre to their titles; but my reverence for the peerage must depend on the *quality* of the materials of which it is composed, and it is from my veneration for this branch of the legislature I assert, that its dignity cannot survive its purity. It is already surcharged with offal, and will not bear any farther addition, without manifest danger to its existence, and that of the monarchy. It is from the sincerest affection for both; it is that their permanency may be assured, and their respective excellencies descend to future times; it is that the country which I love, may be preserved from uproar and civil tumult, that this strong, and I trust effectual remonstrance has been addressed to a man, whose scandalous and expensive levities are unhappily of a nature, to make us loath' and detest royalty: whose conduct has excited alarm and disgust throughout the nation, and whose excesses have been brought more forcibly to our view, by the history of the times, and that at a moment, when the country, defrauded and deserted by a German despot, whose execrable name ought to be erased and torn from the list of sovereigns by the common hangman, provoked the most temperate and best affected men in the kingdom to inquire, with anger and disdain,

IF PRINCES HAVE A PRIVILEGE TO BE SCOUNDREL ?

Well may the republicans repose upon their arms and boast that their work will be done by the Princes of the blood!— Well may the partizans of Mr. Paine, triumph in the vices of courts, and look forward with confidence to the extermination of monarchy—it is by transactions so foul and dishonorable;—it is by a conduct so scandalous and disgraceful, that the peace of society and the very existence of Governments are endangered. It is shameful and unpardonable, that those who are selected from the general mass, and elevated to the highest honors with stipends ample and munificent even to prodigality, for the important and dignified purpose of enforcing obedience to the laws, should be the first to violate them, and encourage by their example, every excess of uproar and wild riot.

Those who would offer in excuse for such licence and disorder, that there is *one* moral for courts, and *another* for the people, are not aware of the mischief that may result from a distinction so degrading to both, and which is no less repugnant to reason, than it is offensive to virtue. In matters of morality and right, mankind ought to be on a par, and every attempt to weaken, efface, or deſtroy this ſalutary, this happy, this glorious equality, the only one worthy of our emulation! argues equal profligacy and impudence—It was eaſy to foreſee from the principles and conduct of thoſe whom his Royal Highneſs admitted to his confidence and table in early life, what would be the ſad iſſue of a ſelection ſo injudicious and ſo very incompatible with his elevated rank in ſociety?

The influence which ſuch men would obtain over his infant and uninformed mind, was a natural conſequence, which however it may awaken our compaſſion for the paſt, or our fears for the future, ought not to ſurpriſe us. I do not enter into the hiſtory of his amours, nor into the very equivocal character of the lady, whom one part of what is called the faſhionable world, conſidered as his *miſtreſs*, and avoided; and whom the other, more ſervile and corrupt, regarded as a woman whoſe careſſes were regiſtered, and legaliſed in heaven, if not on earth, and whoſe mockery of a ſacrament and of the laws gave her a paſſport to that ſociety from which women leſs exceptionable were excluded—It will be ſaid, perhaps, that thoſe, whoſe ſcruples could be ſo eaſily removed, and who could find in ſuch a ſalvo, an excuſe for viſiting Mrs. Fitzherbert, were not very nice in their morals, or, as the Prince expecting, (as a tribute of reſpect to himſelf) that the Lady ſhould be of every party, where he was invited, their ſenſe of decorum was ſacrificed to their vanity.—I cannot diſcuſs ſuch queſtions; nor am I caſuiſt enough to comprehend ſuch diſtinctions. —It is only on plain and incontrovertible facts, that my judgment can decide; and from the evidence before me I feel no difficulty in declaring, that thoſe, whoſe ſervility could deſcend to ſuch a condition, were baſe and abject in the extreme; while the man, who could exact ſuch a conceffion, as the price of his company, or as a tribute due to his rank, manifefted an arrogance of temper, and a contempt of decency, highly incompatible with that refpect which he owes to the nation, and which, (confidering the influence he derives from his character in the State) cannot be reprobated with too much feverity. I am however willing that this tranfaction, difreputable and connected as it is, with that which might have endangered his fucceffion, if it had been honeftly inveftigated, fhould be buried in oblivion, but I will never fubfcribe to the juftice or expediency of adminiftering to vice and folly, or of fupporting expenfive eftablifhments, which impoverifh the country, while they enervate its character, and corrupt its morals. It was with a view to reclaim his Royal Highnefs from bad company, that the letters figned Neptune were addreffed to him in 1784, and when at the diftance of feven years, the fcandalous adventure at Newmarket proved, that admonitions were without effect; when it appeared that bad habits and bad example, had taken ftrong and deep root in a mind, on the purity of which the fate of millions might hereafter depend, it was furely juftifiable in the writer who figns himfelf Legion, to expofe in all the feverity of language, a conduct in which guilt and meannefs, difputing the fuperiority, aimed at depriving the nation of its faireft hope and promife!—It is unneceffary to fay, what ought to have been the reflections of the Prince at thefe different periods, when the author of thofe letters, unconnected as he was, and ever will remain with every defcription of party and cabal, admonifhed his Royal Highnefs of his danger, and predicted what has happened.—Matter of much more immediate import to the nation, than his countenancing faction and every fpecies of profligate libertinifm, has occurred; principles have been manifefted, which it behoves us to refift, and which announce, as little judgment as good faith in the quarter, from whence they originated.

A credit moſt ſhamefully abuſed, and finally exhauſted, has compelled the Prince of Wales to requeſt Parliament to increaſe his income, not altogether for the purpoſe of defraying the expences of an enlarged eſtabliſhment, but to diſcharge incumbrances which he pledged himſelf in 1787, ſhould never be contracted—The amount of the debt, enormous as it is, does not ſtartle us ſo much, as the indecency of *breaking* his word to the nation, and if he has obſerved ſuch little good faith as *Prince of Wales*, what right have we to expect a conduct more correct and more conſonant with his obligations, when he aſſumes a more exalted ſtation in the country? I will not abandon facts for conjecture, by aſking if his Royal Highneſs would have applied to Parliament for ſo much of the public money, if he could have taken it *without?* Neither will I inquire, if, while he conforms in appearance to the conſtitution, he conſiders the people as his Bankers, and their repreſentatives as their clerks?—All that I contend for is, that the country will be equally wronged and inſulted, whether thoſe debts are diſcharged through the medium of the Houſe of Commons, or by a mandate addreſſed in the firſt inſtance to the clerks at the Exchequer.

Another matter for conſideration is, that this ſecond application, unlike the firſt, was not accompanied by any aſſurance either from the King or his Royal Highneſs, that no future demand of the kind ſhould be repeated—This omiſſion is certainly extraordinary and merits obſervation. —It warrants a belief, that the parties conſider themſelves entitled to call on the extra bounty of the nation whenever they think proper, or (which muſt be matter of infinite pain and humiliation to his Royal Highneſs) that the assurance was not given, because its veracity could not be relied on; Our experience unhappily gives equal force and validity to both suppositions, and with such clear and explicit evidence of the facts upon record, it was the duty of a British House of Commons, and I am sure it would have been more consistent with its honor, and infinitely more manly and dignified, to have said,

"*Thus far shall ye go, and no farther.*"

It was incumbent on the representatives of the people to have prescribed bounds to unfeeling prodigality and to insatiate avarice, and not to have given IMPUNITY to the insolence, of the one, and to the rapacity of the other. Such a conduct would have restored the House of Commons to that credit and confidence with the nation, without which, its duration will at best be precarious, and rather endured, than approved, and which conduct, would have been a complete answer to petitions for reform. The only question to be considered, is not such as the Chancellor of the Exchequer was constrained to submit to the judgment of parliament, and on which many will decide, who have little right to give an opinion, either from their capacity, or their rectitude.———It is not, whether the Prince of Wales shall have an annual income of 65,000, or 125,000 pounds, and be permitted to call occasionally, for temporary aids, but whether the former sum in addition to the Duchy of Cornwall (*a*) was not a very ample provision

---

(*a*) Instead of adhering to what alone the Commons of Great Britain were bound to notice, and to which alone they should have confined themselves—instead of taking that line, which was pointed out by the message in 1787, and authorised by a departure from it in 1795—An attempt was made to entangle and perplex a constitutional question of considerable magnitude, with questions of law, and to convert Parliament into a Court of Chancery, to hear an improbable charge of embezzlement or misapplication of property

and fully adequate to support the splendor of an individual of his exalted rank and pretentions, and whether, when

in truſt, preferred on behalf of a minor againſt his father.—I will not diſtreſs the feelings, nor alarm the fears of thoſe gentlemen, who would have degraded the repreſentative dignity, by queſtions, which can only be diſcuſſed with propriety and effect, in a Court of Law or Equity—Their motives for ſo extraordinary a departure from their line of duty, may poſſibly have been perfectly honorable and diſintereſted; but it is a queſtion of legiſlation, and not of law, which they were called upon to decide, and a queſtion which very materially relates to the honor and ſecurity of the Royal Family on the one ſide, and to the preſervation of the conſtitution on the other, for if we loſe it, where ſhall we ſeek another? Reſtored to its purity, where can we find its equal? The queſtion to be conſidered, is not whether the Duchy of Cornwall belongs in fee to the Prince of Wales—It is not whether he holds it by Military Tenure, or by the Peers Tenure, or whether the King, having received the rents during the minority of the Prince, ſhould be called upon to refund, what, after deducting the expences of his education and maintenance, would be no object either to the nation, or to his Royal Highneſs, but whether the Prince of Wales ſhall come to Parliament for a million of the public money, whenever he thinks proper; and whether it is honeſt or grateful in thoſe, whom the country ſupports in ſplendor and magnificence, to run riot, and waſte its property, in profligate and expenſive pleaſures, in which decency, taſte, and œconomy, are equally ſacrificed? It is not a frivolous diſpute between a guardian and his ward, of little import even to the parties, and of much leſs to the nation, but a matter involving in it a variety of ſerious and national conſiderations—It is whether the morals of the country ſhall be preſerved or deſtroyed—It is whether thoſe who have dared to offer them every poſſible inſult, ſhall be allowed to proceed in their diſgraceful career with impunity?—It is in fact whether we will any longer ſubmit to the inſolent licentiouſneſs of thoſe, who ſeem by their conduct to imagine, that we are created for their ſole uſe and convenience, and fit only to adminiſter to their vices and neceſſities?—I can pity and forgive the imbecillity that is flattered by ſuch an idea, but the guilt that would act in conformity to it, deſerves chaſtiſement, and ſhall find no quarter.

I will ſpare his Royal Highneſs the painful recital of tranſactions, which are no leſs repugnant to his obligations to ſociety, than they have been ruinous and diſgraceful to himſelf. I wiſh to draw a veil between our indignant and offended ſight, and thoſe diſreputable ſcenes, which have finally deprived him and his brothers of that affection and reſpect, which were ſpon-

settled on him, it was decent or just in his Royal Highness to have exceeded it?

taneously bestowed and fondly continued, while the most distant hope was entertained of amendment or contrition. I will not comment on their disgraceful history, nor dwell on the shameless profligacy, that has dared to appear at a place of public resort in defiance of all decency and decorum, with a public actress, an acknowledged prostitute, at whose door, two centinels were often tatiously placed, as if the guilt of the Lady, and the depravity of her Lover were not already sufficiently conspicuous—That such an indecency should have been offered, has more in it to offend than to surprise us; the wonder is, that the company assembled at Brighton should have submitted to the insult, but, "*I will not spread the compost on the weeds to make them ranker,*" neither will I enlarge on the rash and inconsiderate levity, of appropriating to her use the Royal carriages, and attendants in Royal liveries, allowed him by the munificence of the nation to support the splendor of his rank, and not to insult the morals and good sense of the country—Flagrant, and indecent as this conduct unquestionably is, its turpitude is lost in the magnitude of other, and more important considerations, which the criminal and inexplicable profligacy of Princes (as if a fatality attended them!) press on our attention, and which I will defy the most cool and collected mind to contemplate, without gloom and alarm. This brother, who has thrown much random and incoherent censure on ministers, to which their public conduct, gives a flat contradiction, seems to consider the restrictions intended to be imposed on future Princes of Wales, as a personality levelled at his brother—allowing this to be the fact, what must futurity think of THAT brother, who reduced the legislature to the necessity of such a measure? The question for consideration is not, Whether the Heir Apparent shall have a larger or a lesser establishment—It is not whether he shall be at liberty to contract debts, beyond his ability to discharge; but whether he shall be allowed to persevere in a line of conduct, which may endanger the peace of the country, and finally consign him to beggary and exile? This is in fact the question that Parliament is called upon to decide, and as it involves in it the ease, comfort, and security of every individual in the empire, it behoves the House of Peers to whom the Commons may possibly refer the important consideration, and to whose rectitude of conduct the nation looks up with hope and confidence, to give it the attention it deserves, and to stand between their country and ruin. Woe be to Parliament and to the British Empire, whenever the former has the guilt or imprudence to act in opposition to the general sense of the latter; nor can it be too strongly impressed on the memory of both, that the prodigality which accomplished the ruin of the Court of Versailles, led also

This is the only point of view in which parliament can with propriety confider the application, that has been recently made; it is the only one, on which I can defcend to join iffue with thofe, who are difpofed to fupport the claim. Honor, policy and gratitude forbade its being made in any form or fhape, and leaft of all by juggle, and were I difpofed to enjoy a malignant triumph over thofe who have unfortunately lowered themfelves by this meafure in the public eftimation, I am moft amply furnifhed with the means; but feeling for declining age, and commifferating all the moral infirmities annexed to it, I will fpare majefty the reproach which it appears to have incurred, and leave the country to decide on the extreme indifcretion that has provoked a difcuffion fo unfavorable to the caufe of monarchy. As joint bondfman with his fon, he would have done well to have preferved his Royal Highnefs from the ignominy of his prefent fituation: It was his intereft, and furely it was his duty, to have fhewn in times like the prefent, full of peril

---

to the complete Bankruptcy and extinction of Royalty in France. The courfe which the legiflature of this country has to fteer, may be difficult and perilous, but with fuch vifible and numerous beacons on every fide, there will be infanity or fomething worfe, in miftaking it.—The unexampled diftrefs of the times—the frequent and heavy demands for money to profecute the war to an honorable conclufion, forbid moft eloquently, and moft forcibly, any improvident, or wanton expenditure of the public treafure, and efpecially in favor of an individual, whofe claim to the generofity of the nation is denied, and with whofe conduct fuch ftrong and univerfal difatisfaction has been univerfally expreffed—It behoves Parliament to reflect well on the probable confequences of their prefent proceedings.—There is wifdom in deliberation, and it behoves them to confider, if what they intend for kindnefs, may not prove the reverfe? It is poffible, that much mifchief may refult from a miftaken and ill-timed generofity, not only to the Sovereign whom it is their duty to refpect, and to his offspring, whom they would fupport and cherifh in a ftyle fuitable to their exalted rank in fociety, but to the country whofe tranquillity they are bound by the ftrongeft of all poffible ties, to preferve.

and of danger, that a king can be faithful to his engagements.

Strong as thefe animadverfions may appear to weak and timid men; to men who mean well, and think right, but who are afraid to fay what they think; Offenfive and democratic as thefe animadverfions may be reprefented, by the fervile and corrupt; I will venture to affert that my loyalty has much lefs of that alloy in it, than thofe who flatter and miflead the Prince. —I love royalty, but it muft have its appendages, as well as its trappings, or its claim to refpect will be laughed at, and its exiftence endangered—I have been accufed of attacking his Royal Highnefs with indecency, but does the indecency of *my* language equal the indecency of HIS conduct, and is vice in full drefs, and at Court, to be worfhipped? Can birth or titles fanction crime, or give to vice and folly a privilege to infult public morals and to fquander the public money with impunity? Thofe who can anfwer in the affirmative are qualified for an idolatry more filthy and abfurd than that of the Jews, and to fuch worfhip I confign them.—With refpect to the motives that urged me to the publication of the foregoing pages, they are juftified by the occafion that excited them—I really forefee much ferious and not very remote mifchief to the conftitution, unlefs principles of rectitude are fpeedily adopted, and a good example given by thofe, in whom it is infamy to give a bad one, and whenever the figns of amendment appear at Carleton Houfe, and his Royal Highnefs acknowledges by his *conduct*, what he owes to his country, I will be as ready to applaud, as I have been to cenfure.—He is no longer juvenile, and he will do well to remember, that what are FOLLIES at Twenty are VICES at Forty.

It muft however be left to time to difcover what effect thefe letters will have on the mind of the perfon, to whom they are addressed;—it is possible that he may regard them as the expedient of a necessitous scribbler to obtain temporary relief; it is even possible, that his Royal Highness may have *smiled* at animadversions, which ought to have excited other sensations than those of merriment; he may even have branded the pamphlet, as the miserable catchpenny of an author, who availing himself of a popular topic, would answer and refute his own assertions;—if such *should* have been the observations of the Prince, to the person *whom he requested would read the letter to him,* and if the idea that I am venal, or that I am profligate enough to write, on *both sides* of the question, should afford any consolation to his *royal* mind, he is right welcome to every enjoyment it can afford him; I certainly shall not envy him, either his feelings or his judgment. There are those about the Prince, who may suggest and foster such an idea, while others may represent the author as a man tainted with democracy, and disaffected to the throne. To his Royal Highness and those of the *former* description it may be a sufficient answer to their opinions and conjectures, to say, that superior to the infamy of writing for hire, and having no object in view but to preserve the constitution from the danger with which it is menaced by the conduct of the male branches of the Royal Family, I have given the profits of this publication, whatever they may be, to the Publisher: and to those of the latter description who may be disposed to brand me as democratic, I have only to lament that an odium should of late become attached to what happily forms a very considerable ingredient in our admirable constitution, and which should be cherished—not decried, at a moment when it is attempted to supplant our national democracy by a wild and ruthless democracy subversive of morals, religion, and all public and private security—I have neither spleen nor resentment to gratify against the Royal Family; on the contrary, I have much affection and respect for them, but their smiles, unless in approbation of a conduct which I feel to be laudable and just, have no charms; and as to their frowns, it is impossible they can disturb or affect me—I am ready to pay every homage, that is due to the sovereign and his family—Their rank in the constitution certainly gives them a claim to affection and respect, but it is only a conduct correspondent with their station, that can legitimate and ratify the claim; allegiance, respect, friendship, and all the various duties, which men living together in society, owe to each other, are relative and reciprocal: dependent on the fidelity by which they act towards each other, and no longer binding on *one* side, than they are accurately observed and faithfully fulfilled on the *other:* —In this country, where *men* and *things* are considered as distinct, and where the union of the *office* and the *man*, is conditional; where Majesty is (as it ought to be every where else) the collected force, and wisdom of the nation; it is necessary, that the Throne should be supported; not by terror, or by the blaze of exterior and unprofitable splendor, but by affection.—To be dependent on a blind and senseless superstition, subject to the caprice of opinion, and the fluctuations of time, would be at once disgraceful and insecure; the dignity and preservation of the Throne, must, as well as its origin, be derived from the operations of reason, and the test of experience; for the only safe and honorable avenue to the heart, is by the understanding; all other props are irrational, hazardous, and precarious; more likely to accelerate mischief, than to prevent it, and to which a mind, weak, or vicious in the extreme, only would have recourse.—The province of Royalty is to vivify, cheer, and exhilarate; not to awe, dazzle, and petrify.—Its powers, to be respected and obeyed, must be attractive, not repellant;

an authority thus regulated, confirms, and confolidates itfelf, by its own weight; it claims the adoration of mankind as a right, not as a favor, and affures to the Sovereign, that loyalty and obedience, which he can never acquire, or retain by violence—In a word, our love of *monarchy* is irrevocable;—it is a fixture in the mind, and cannot be difplaced; but our love of the *monarch* muft ever remain a contingency on his conduct and capacity, to be fufpended, continued, or withdrawn, as circumftances may require. A wife man, will not difpute the validity of fuch a tenure, much lefs will he hazard it;—a good one, would not wifh to hold a fceptre on any other, and it is on the unqueftionable evidence of Englifh Hiftory I affert, that the Englifh Nation will never fuffer a bad man to hold it on *any* conditions.—Such are the doctrines and fuch the principles, that ought to be inftilled into the mind of a Britifh Prince; they are at once wholefcme and conftitutional;—they are connected with his honor and his happinefs, and fo intimately blended with the peace, order, and fecurity of Government, that to fpurn or neglect them, is to endanger the whole fabric of civil fociety.—Such are the precepts, which a Britifh fovereign is bound, no lefs by intereft than by duty to follow; and if thofe who were charged with the education of the Prince of Wales, in early life, had executed the truft repofed in them, with that fidelity which was due to his Royal Highnefs, their Sovereign and their country, the credit of the one would not have been impaired, nor the tranquillity of the other difturbed, by a difcuffion as painful to the Nation, as it is perfonally difreputable to the parties concerned.

I am not confcious, that this definition of monarchy, and of the obligations of the monarch, contain any thing offenfive, or hoftile to either—I know my mind to be perfectly free from every taint of difaffection, and that the fentiments I have advanced, are not only warranted by thofe maxims of equity and common fenfe, which form the bafis of al free governments, but that they are juftified by the maxims of the Britifh conftitution, to which I will remain fteadily and unalterably, attached to the laft moment of my exiftence.

It is from that ftrong and unaffected attachment, which I feel for the conftitution; it is from a fincere and ardent defire, that it may be perpetuated to the very end of time, that I have reprobated with all the force and animation or language, the conduct of a man to whofe fortunes we are attached, and whofe very errors may be the fource of infinite mifchief and diftrefs to millions. If his conduct had been lefs flagitious, I would have been lefs fevere; if it had been exemplary, I would have been the loudeft in his praife! but with a ftake in the country to the full as valuable, to the full as important, and as neceffary to MY comfort, felicity, and fecurity, as the diadem is to the peace, furety, and honor of his Royal Father, I felt myfelf called upon to reprobate, what has a direct and manifeft tendency to endanger the whole, and entail diforder and ruin on the nation. It is a miftaken idea, and as falfe in theory as it would prove pernicious in practice, that the conduct of the Heir Apparent fhould be exempted from the cognizance, cenfure, or obfervation of the people; the reverfe of the propofition is the fact; the character of his Royal Highnefs partakes of the nature of public and private property: it is an extended common, reaching from one extremity of the empire to the other, in the prefervation of which, every individual has a common right, and common intereft. Thofe of the prince are greater, not only from that immediate perfonal concern which he poffeffes, but from the flattering and animating diftinction, of being guardian of his own ho-

K

nor, not for the exclusive benefit of himself, but in trust for the happiness, security, and independence of the whole kingdom! This is the relation in which his Royal Highness stands; and considering him in this point of view, every deviation from the rule of right, is a matter of public concern, and authorises censure or complaint, in proportion to the injury or mischief, that may result from it. I disclaim all personal rancor against the Prince—it is impossible that I can have cause for any; but even if I had, my temper and my habits forbid me to avail myself of it. It is therefore on the broad and strong ground of public right, that I have delivered, not only my own sentiments, but those of the entire nation. It is from the interest that I have in a constitution to which I am attached, not only from a full conviction of its many excellencies, but from a love of that order which modulates, preserves, and harmonizes civil society; of that order, on which our liberties and fortunes depend, and which we are bound to cherish and respect, that I have censured a conduct, reprobated by every individual in the empire, and which is acknowledged to have a direct and immediate tendency to excite and authorise public discontents. Had his Royal Highness been instructed in those obligations which he owes to the country; had he been taught to consider himself as an individual, on whom distinction is bestowed, to excite him to an honorable discharge of the station he holds, and of the duties he may hereafter be called upon to execute, there would probably have been no occasion for these animadversions, the severity of which is justified by the magnitude of the danger with which we are threatened, from an obstinate, not to say vicious, perseverance in those errors, from which every attempt to reclaim him, has hitherto proved fruitless. To urge in extenuation of his conduct, that he has been *ill-counselled*, is an insult at once to his understanding and the common-fenfe of mankind; for having alfo been WELL-COUNSELLED, and being of an age to comprehend the force and extent of his obligations to fociety, with a mind capable of difcriminating right from wrong, he is without the fhadow of an excufe, for what would be criminal and flagitious even in men, whofe irregularities could not be of any mifchievous confequence to the general interefts of the community: but there feems to be a fatality attending him, as lamentable, as it is unexampled. His hiftory excites a conflict in the mind whenever it occurs, and my anger is checked by my humanity, in reflecting on the haplefs deftiny which has marked his progrefs through life. That the Prince has been ill-advifed, is a truth univerfally admitted, and as univerfally regretted, nor has he been more happy in his advocates, than in his friendfhips; the former is likely to prove as mifchievous to his fame, as the latter have been to his fortune. The one has entailed on him dishonor—the other poverty; whilst both of them have the effrontery to pretend an attachment to the object, whom they have ruined and difgraced! One of this latter defcription, comes forward in fupport of the Prince, not from affection to his Royal Highnefs, but avowedly to promote mifchief; the vices of his profeffion are added to the follies of youth, and *whether it is apples of difcord that he diftributes, or windows that he breaks*, the gentleman is equally diverted, for his view is not to benefit the Heir Apparent, but to embarrafs government, by entangling a queftion fufficiently clear, with law fubtleties. The gentleman acknowledges, that he is not ftimulated by affection to royalty, but by hatred to the minifter; his wifh, he fays, is merely to worry, teafe, and perplex. The Prince of Wales has only the *chance* of the iffue being favorable to his caufe: He is merely a fecondary confideration, and rather the inftrument of intentional mifchief in the hands of this quibbler, than an object of compassion, while the gentleman, anticipating with malignant joy, the confusion that he fancies his labors will create, looks forwards to distinction and reward from a change in his Majesty's councils!—I disclaim all such motives, and hold in equal contempt and abhorrence, all those who have the guilt or folly to avow them—These are not times for dissention, but UNION; and his Royal Highness will do well to reflect on the additional odium, disgrace, and infamy, that will inevitably result, from his following the pernicious and malignant councils of those, who advise him to prosecute his Majesty, or rather the nation, for arrears of rents pretended to be due from the duchy of Cornwall, after he had authorised Mr. Anstruther to declare that "*he would leave all matters, relative to his establishment, and the payment of his debts, to the wisdom and discretion of parliament, and that he desired nothing more, than what the country might cordially be induced, to think, he ought to have*"—It was in consequence of this apparent submission to the pleasure of the legislature, and which was peculiarly due from his Royal Highness to the country, offended and irritated as it was by his extraordinary conduct, that an income was allotted, sufficiently large to provide for the payment of his debts, and for his own domestic comfort; and having obtained this munificent provision from the bounty of the nation, in consequence of the assurance solemnly and publicly given, of a perfect acquiescence with whatever should be granted, I will leave his Royal Highness to judge of the decency, the propriety, and rectitude of again violating his promise, by making a demand on the public purse for a sum little short of THREE HUNDRED THOUSAND POUNDS! exclusive of interest accumulated during his minority, and which they pretend must also be paid. Is this the return that the counsellors of his Royal Highness advise him to make, to the generosity and clemency of his country for having liberated him from debts, wantonly contracted a second time?—Is this the gratitude, with which he promised *" to acquiesce with whatever the country might cordially be induced to think he ought to have,"* and will such counsellors have the effrontery to contend, that they have the honor and interest of his Royal Highness at heart, when they recommend a measure, and start a claim (without any colourable pretext either in equity or necessity, for the Prince is no longer embarrassed with debts) which in private life would be considered as tantamount to swindling, and stamped as infamous? Have these men, so little regard for the honor of the Prince as to engage him to violate his word a THIRD TIME?—Are they so little acquainted with his interests, and have they so little regard for his domestic happiness, as to involve him in litigation with his father; or would they make his father only a pretext, to plunder the nation of near half'a million, which, if it could be spared, would be much better applied in purchasing corn for a famished peasantry, and averting the calamities to be apprehended from the scarcity with which the country is unhappily afflicted, than in administering to the prodigality of Carleton House, liberated as it is from all embarrassment, its establishments reduced, and having no longer either distress, or pecuniary difficulties, to urge in excuse? Is it then decreed, that the Heir Apparent shall give his confidence to those only, who mislead, or betray him, and have they the folly and impudence to imagine, that the nation will submit to be the dupe, or victim, of their treachery or ignorance? Let the law luminary who is supposed to direct the counsels at Carleton House, and the two gentlemen in the House of Commons, to whom *alone*, his Royal Highness confesses himself obliged, say if they dare, to what purposes this enormous sum is *intended* to be applied. The triumvirate is not very respectable,

I confess; but equivocal as their testimony might be on any other occasion, on this it would be less liable to suspicion, and perhaps entitled to credit, even against the strong evidence of recorded falsehood. At all events, before the Prince of Wales can institute with propriety or decency, any process at law against the King, for the recovery of a sum so enormously large, and for which, if awarded in his favor, the country may be called upon to advance, it is incumbent on his Royal Highness to state to the nation, the uses to which it is meant to appropriate so considerable a portion of its wealth; and this declaration is the more necessary, not only from his having obtained a very magnificent establishment, and complete emancipation from debt, but from his having pledged himself to *remain perfectly satisfied with whatever parliament will allow him.* Thus bound to an acquiescence, by an engagement too solemnly made, and too publicly given, to be violated with impunity, his Royal Highness will do well to reflect on the advice he has received, and to peremptorily reject the pernicious counsels of men, whose element appears to be vexatious litigation, and who can have no respect either for their Sovereign, his son, or their country, by wishing to involve them in a process at law, which can answer no other purpose, than to inspire hatred and distrust, where mutual affection and confidence ought to exist, and to indispose them towards each other. An advocate for the Prince of another description, enters the list; but instead of discussing the right and expediency of paying the debts of the Prince; instead of refuting the charge of a breach of promise, or justifying the violation of a solemn engagement, contracted with the nation; through the medium of parliament, boldly declares that all such considerations are trifling and un-important, and even questions the loyalty and good-manners of the man, who from a love of order and of equity, has condemned so wanton and so flagrant a departure from the maxims of policy and justice. The humanity of the judge who passes sentence on a convicted felon, may with equal propriety, be arraigned; and if hereditary, or acquired rank, is to give impunity to vice or folly, the equality of our laws is destroyed, and legislation dishonored. A third man of buckram, and a no less animated defender of his Royal Highness, offers his "high station" as a sufficient apology for the sum total of all his transgressions, past, present and to come; this wholesale dealer in right and wrong has however given me an opportunity to join issue with him on a question of considerable importance to the Prince, and of much greater to the nation, which my respect for both, will not allow me to neglect; the writer alluded to, acknowledges that "*whatever undermines royalty and degrades the station of the Prince, delivers up the state of the subject to dishonor and danger, if not to downfall:*" In this, I most cordially agree, and thus agreed, I request the favor of him to say, who it is that "*undermines royalty?*" those Princes who degrade their station by a gross and unpardonable licentiousness, or the man who would awaken them to a sense of their duty, and compel them to act like HONEST MEN? If this question had occurred to my opponent, I do not think, that he would have hazarded an aphorism that makes so strongly against him. Such advocates are sufficient to ruin a good cause, and I am sure they cannot benefit a bad one.

The arguments of this gentleman in support of his assertions, prove very little in favor, either of his capacity or principles, but they demonstrate to a certainty, in whose service he is enlisted: such reasoners should be taught better logic, and their employers better maxims.—They say, that to reprehend princes for their profusion and debaucheries is to "*assassinate royalty;*" to expose the profligacy of that opposition, which has brought all opposition, if not into contempt, at least into disrepute (*a*), is to be the "*minion of*

(*a*) Let the measures of ministers be canvassed with freedom; let them even be scrutinized with severity: those who mean well and act well, have nothing to fear from the exercise of a right, which is meant to check presumptuous ignorance, and profligate ambition. It is their duty to submit to precautions dictated by wisdom, and justified by experience, for power will dazzle the strongest, and corrupt the best disposed minds; but let the justice that condemns negligence or abuse, be as ready to applaud desert; let those who investigate the conduct of ministers, prove by their candor and discernment, the purity of their motives, and the importance of their functions; they will then be considered as the extra-guardians of our laws and liberties; as honorary members of the government, whose proceedings they superintend; and they will prevent by their example, as well as by their vigilance, the mischiefs that might result from the guilt or imbecility of men, whom fortune, not merit, may have raised to situations for which nature never designed them. An opposition animated by such motives, and adhering to such principles, is entitled by the courtesy of the constitution, not only to our esteem, but to a portion of our confidence, and instances have occurred, where it has had claims to our gratitude. Such are the genuine features of an opposition worthy of support, and which can alone correct the blunders of weak, and counteract the designs of corrupt ministers. When men descend to the miserable expedient of seeking, through the medium of clubs, taverns, and field-meetings, a popularity as disreputable as it is transitory and precarious;—when they declaim, with as little decency as truth, on their own virtues, and the vices of ministers;—when, under the pretence of commemorating an election-triumph, they assemble a promiscuous multitude to hear fulsome and preconcerted panegyrics, rehearsed by each other in rotation, on the purity of each other's motives, and the splendor of each other's talents, we expect no good from their efforts, and only question the truth of eulogiums which are pronounced by those, who are the objects of them; but when, like wary gamesters, they watch for the moment of inebriety, when the intellects of their companions are debilitated by wine, and their judgments are as palsied as their hands, to seduce them into an unqualified applause of every past, and a solemn promise of support, to every future enterprise, the mischief they intend us is no longer problematical, and we are insensibly put on our guard by the very means they employ to surprise us; we then perceive that it is no longer that dignified opposition, which would be at once the boast and security of the British constitution, but a faction whose object is to ob-

the minister." Here the enigma is unravelled: it is not my disaffection to the throne, but to Mr. Fox and his friends, that has given offence; my loyalty to the Sovereign would not have been questioned, but for my hostility to those who endeavour to perplex the measures of his government, with a view to force themselves into his councils, and usurp the administration of affairs; it is not an affection for the Prince of Wales, or for Royalty, or for the Cause of Monarchy, that has provoked all this calumny and misrepresentation, but despair at the little prospect of that party, ever being admitted again into power, which has entailed disgrace on all parties; it is in fact the miserable effort of a faction, degraded, scattered and despised, to regain that credit with the Nation, which the honor, dignity, and independence of the empire required should be totally and irrevocably withdrawn.—His Royal Highness on this occasion is nothing more than the stalking horse of men who having formerly made him the instrument of their ambition, would now, if they dare, notwithstanding he has spurned them, unite and make common cause with him for their mutual redemption. This lefthanded champion for the Prince, appears to be as ill informed of my situation and pursuits in life, as he is inaccurate in his conclusions, or he would not have accused me of being "*the minion of the minister, or of having a design to subvert the monarchy*"—My language and sentiments should exempt me from such reproaches, and the public opinion is decidedly in my favour, when I assert, that monarchy and nobility, have much more to apprehend from

tain power by any means, however abject, and on any terms, however atrocious; and which assumes the mask of public virtue, with a view to impose on those who consider professions as demonstrations, and assertions as facts

the profligacy of Princes, than from the mifchievous efforts of thofe whofe object it is to throw the country into confufion.

I really did not expect that any man would have had the temerity to advance fuch charges againft a pamphlet every line of which pleads loudly in favor of that conftitution, to which I have been attached from my infancy, with which I am refolved to ftand or fall, and in defence of which, I will ever come forward, whether its exiftence is endangered by indifcretion or turpitude in the Royal Family; by the clamors of party; the incapacity of minifters; or the feditious attempts of pennylefs and unprincipled incendiaries. The loyalty of an Englifhman is due to the laws and conftitution of his country, not to individuals, and until thofe laws and that conftitution authorife a wanton violation of decency and right, he is not only juftified, but called upon by the intereft which he has in their prefervation, to detect, expofe, and punifh whatever tends to bring either, into hazard or difrepute. With refpect to my purfuits in life, I have nothing to hope, and certainly nothing to fear, from the favor, or the anger, of thofe, who are the objects of this remonftrance: my mind, prepared for the worft, has nothing to apprehend from the events of thefe ftrange, difjointed times; and to whatever fum, an income, competent to the fimplicity of my life and manners, may be hereafter reduced, I am refolved to live within it—It is the barrier to my independence; and independence, it is well known, is the beft fecurity that mankind can have for their integrity.—

SECOND POSTSCRIPT.

TENTH EDITION.

IT was generally reported on the 1st ult. that a message of a conciliatory nature would be sent by the Prince of Wales to the House of Commons, the chief object of which was to allay the strong ferment which a message from the king had excited throughout the country, and which could not possibly have had any other effect than that of indisposing the public mind against his Royal Highness and against Monarchy. The forgiving temper of the nation will always incline it to receive with equal pleasure and alacrity, any thing in the shape of an apology, and when the magnitude of the affront, that had been offered, and the principle in which it most probably originated, are considered, it was surely reasonable to expect that an atonement proportioned to the insult would have been made.—Hence the full credit that was instantly given to the report, and (disdaining to investigate motives) what evidently resulted from fear, was generously assigned to contrition. If this well-grounded expectation had been realised, the ill humor provoked by insolence and injustice, would have subsided, and the odium which eclipses his Royal Highness, to a darkness worse than total, would have been removed, but our hopes were no sooner raised than they were destroyed, and the delusion became evident to all, but those who had a legal right to defeat and punish it. The message had nothing conciliatory, but the extreme mildness with which it was delivered, which being natural to the manners of the man, the merit, if any, is trifling, and belongs entirely to Mr. Anstruther. This gentleman, it seems, was authorised to inform the House of Commons that " *the wish of his Royal Highness on the occasion was entirely to consult the wisdom of Parliament; that he desired nothing but what the country might cordially be induced to think he ought to have; and finally that he left all matters relative to the regulation of his establishment and the payment of his debts, to the wisdom and discretion of Parliament.*" If these are to be considered as words, of course, like " *honorable,*" " *right honorable,*" " *illustrious,*" " *noble,*" and many others of the same description, I have no objection to their obtaining that currency which the ridiculous and dangerous refinement of the times has unhappily given to perverted language; I am too feeble to stem this torrent of fraud alone, yet inadequate as my strength may be to resist its force, I will make the effort, and leave it to the prudence and virtue of my country to succour, or abandon me—but if these words are to be received agreeable to their common import, and in the only sense in which they are intelligible to men of sober and correct minds, I deny that they afford the most distant proof of either condescension, shame, remorse, humiliation, or justice. It is publicly reported, that council is retained to prosecute the claim of his Royal Highness to the arrears of rent for the Duchy of Cornwall. Those who advise such a prosecution, are not aware of the consequences that may result from such a measure, while sober, well disposed men, without examining the breach of faith to the country in the first instance, may be tempted to ask for WHAT PURPOSE the nation is to be drained of near half a million of its property, after having provided for the payment of his debts, and allotted him an establishment equal to most Soveriegn Princes on the Continent? His Royal Highness, thus amply provided for, and thus exonerated a second time from embarrassments, can have no justifiable motive for taking a sum so enormously large from the country, and it may well be asked, of those who have the criminal indiscretion to council a measure so disreputable to the Prince, if one of the *uses* to which that money is to be applied, is for the formation and maintenance of that party, which they have the folly and indecency to assert will next year effect, under Royal Patronage, a change in his Majesty's councils? If so, the country has an obligation to their efforts which was never intended, and may thank them for putting it on its guard, by the discovery of a design which proves their talent at invention to be infinitely superior to their capacity for execution. I really do not discover any extraordinary forbearance, in submitting to forms, which cannot be violated without imminent personal risque, nor is the promised acquiescence with whatever establishment the wisdom and discretion of Parliament shall prescribe, entitled to much admiration, when we reflect on the impossibility of obtaining it by any other means. I really do not perceive any great condescension, in agreeing to accept as a *favor*, what it was very well known, would never have been granted on any other condition, nor can I discover any thing very moderate, or conciliatory in a demand for SEVEN HUNDRED THOUSAND POUNDS, which leaves only to those who are to advance a sum most shamefully enormous, the *mode* by which it is to be raised, much less does it establish his claim to our confidence or forgiveness, of that, which has diffused a very serious and general alarm throughout the whole country.—What is it in fact, but the History of the Sturdy Beggar, who, finding it more convenient to receive as a *boon*, what he would have exacted by force as a *right*, makes a merit of the concession, and laughs at us while he wrongs us? Surely the nation has a claim to better treatment; nor does it redound to the honor of the Prince, that he should owe more to the compassion and generosity of the country, than it has ever received from his justice or discretion. To be so indebted, is a mendicity of the worst and most odious description. It is full time his Royal Highness should know that, every man in society has duties to fulfil, and obligations to discharge; there is no truth more evident, and the Sovereign and his family have more of both, than any other description of people:—Their restraints are necessarily greater, for exclusive of that respect and obedience, which they owe in common to the laws, it is incumbent on them to give good example, and to discountenance by the purity of their manners in public and in private, every appearance of vice and intemperance—nor is this sobriety of conduct or this sacrifice (if it should be deemed such) required, without an equivalent, and an equivalent of so honorable, so captivating, and so bewitching a nature, as to reflect little credit on the principles and taste of those who can slight or withstand it. It is an equivalent of so rich and splendid a quality, that it appears to every good mind, sufficient to tempt vice to be virtuous, and even avarice to be generous.—I do not allude to the munificent income which supports the pageantry, and rewards the painful decorum of majesty, but to that species of recompense, which is less fluctuating in value, and less perishable in its nature; I allude to that species of compensation which exceeds all estimate, and which is as permanent, as I feel it to be glorious. I mean the love, and adoration of the whole country; I mean that warm, and exhilerating interest, which an entire people always take, in the felicity of those, who *deserve* their affection, and whose plaudits descending to the latest posterity, confer at once, both happiness and fame! If these virtuous and salutary precepts had been instilled into the mind of the Prince and of his brothers, they would not have to lament in the very prime of manhood, their present humbled and degraded situation, but their infancy and earlier years have been shamefully neglected, and corrupt habits and corrupt example, having compleated, what commenced in a faulty and vicious education, we find the eldest of them coming forward, and claiming not only *exemption* from all the wholesome restraints of œconomy and temperance, but *reward* for having violated them, and for having failed in gratitude, duty, and respect to those who contribute to his magnificence—for what other interpretation can honestly be given to the application which has been made to Parliament in 1795, to discharge debts amounting to quadruple the sum that was paid in 1787, under a solemn assurance, that no future demand should be made on the exhausted bounty of the nation?— What else is the offer to "*submit to the wisdom of Parliament the mode for liquidating his debts,*" but a tacit denial of any right on his part to provide for them; and if he had ever considered himself obliged to discharge them, would he have contracted them? I do not know, if the reading of the Prince of Wales has ever extended to natural history, but I find in the conduct of the cuckoo, something that appears to have suggested to his Royal Highness the idea of leaving to others, the task of providing for his incumbrances; if this should be the fact, there may be some ingenuity in the contrivance, but I am sure it argues little policy and less rectitude, and though some of those who pretend to have possessed his confidence, *(a)* may have

---

(a) The capacity of Mr. Sheridan to give advice, cannot well be disputed;—He has been long enough in the school of adversity, to have acquired very competent ideas of discretion, and he is certainly of an age to practice

countenanced the trick by their example, yet if any credit is due to their affertions, their advice was falutary,

what he has learnt, without incurring the reproach of premature sobriety. It is unimportant, however, to inquire into the *extent* of the influence and confidence which that gentleman declares he formerly poffeffed at Carleton Houfe—Nor is it very relative to the queftion before us, to inquire if the advice which he acknowledges he gave to the Heir Apparent was falutary or pernicious—If it was the *former*, we are authorifed to affert from the conduct of the Prince, that the influence of the gentleman over the mind of his Royal Pupil was not fo extenfive as he infinuated; and if it was of the *latter defcription*, we have equally to lament that his Royal Highnefs had *fuch* a Tutor, and was fo apt a fcholar—I am not of a temper to do intentional wrong, nor do I think it juftifiable to hold out a ftring of interrogatories, for the purpofe of queftioning a man until his guilt is difcovered.—Mr. Sheridan declares that he always gave good council to the Prince, and we are bound to believe him until we are fully affured to the contrary—Trufting therefore to his honor for the veracity of the affertion, and admitting that he was fully in the confidence of his Royal Highnefs, as he fays he was, it may not be improper to afk him by whofe advice the Heir Apparent was prevailed upon at the time of the Regency to facrifice the dignity of rank, and in fome degree his honor, by becoming the Proprietor of a News Paper? This tranfaction accompanied as it is by circumftances of meannefs and atrocity which could only have refulted from the moft artful and malignant councils is upon record—The names of thofe who are anfwerable for the punctual payment of the annuity can be produced—The fum paid down on the affignment of the Morning Poft is no fecret, and fufficient evidence were it neceffary, can be produced to prove that the treafury might have had the Paper if it had thought proper to *outbid* his Royal Highnefs. Situated as Mr. Sheridan was at the epoch alluded to; in habits of familiar intercourfe with the Heir Apparent, and in his confidence and fecrets as he declares himfelf to have been, it is impoffible that the *advifer* of this notable expedient could have been *unknown* to him, and he owes it to the country in general, and to his conftituents at Stafford in particular, to reveal the names of the gentlemen, who, at this period, propofed that SIXTY THOUSAND POUNDS, fhould be devoted to the purpofe of purchafing a decided intereft in as many of the Public Prints, as that fum could obtain. Admitting that they would have been purchafed with a liberality correfpondent with the magnificence of their intended Proprietor, and with his known difregard of the *value* of the thing bought, and of the *price* paid for it—We may ftate that the number would have amounted to at leaft a dozen, and it is of that

and as it tended to check a paffion for imitating defects, in preference to perfection, it ought to have been followed.

His Royal Highnefs in that cafe, would have had lefs reafon to regret the intimacies to which he admitted thefe men, and the nation lefs caufe to reprobate their turpitude and effrontery.

The fhameful debt which has angered the nation even to madnefs, would moft probably never have been con-

---

gentleman who is so perfectly acquainted with the nature and influence of our Public Prints, and who owes so very much of his reputation to their indefatigable induftry I will afk, if even his powers are capable to calculate the extent of that force, and the confequences of that superiority which TWELVE NEWSPAPERS in the fervice and pay of Carleton Houfe would have given to the Prince, and his Abettors over the regular Government, when Majefty, in an eclipfe, left it with no other fupport than its virtue and intrepidity?—I will not afk from what fund that fum was to have been furnifhed, nor how much of the prefent debt was incurred in feafting and bribing the defpicable apoftates in both Houfes of Parliament, fome of whom had folemnly pledged themfelves to the minifter to support the only meafures which could preferve the Crown on the head of their Sovereign, and their country, from a Banditti of Bankrupts! Neither will I comment on the rank and vicious fertility of *that* mind, which suggefted the expedient by which the Government of the country was to have been wrefted from those to whom the King had delegated it, and who alone could legally have divefted them of it—The faction thus entrenched, and in a manner secured from all animadverfion, might have abused or perverted the powers of Government with impunity, while the people, debarred, with their own money from the accuftomed channels of free and impartial information, would have contributed to the fraud that robbed them in the firft inftance of their property, and in the second, of that conftitutional check, and control, which affords them perhaps the beft, and moft effectual security againft defpotism— Whenever time fhall reveal the *items* of this fcandalous account, which Parliament is called upon to discharge in the *grofs*, pofterity may poffibly be informed who they were that gave bad advice, and bad example to the deluded, ruined, and haplefs object of this addrefs—The present generation deprived of the means of ample information, is not only required to take affertions upon truft, but to believe them againft the ftrong evidence of appearances, and the ftill ftronger teftimony of its senses!

tracted, and the friends of his Royal Highnefs would have been relieved from the laborious tafk of urging the neceffity of fomething like a fubmiffion on his part, to the pleafure of parliament, and which, from the circumftance of its having been made a fortnight after the application, authorizes an opinion, that it was rather a meafure of neceffity than of choice. This meffage, announced with fo much art and induftry to be of a conciliatory nature, afforded an admirable pretext to many who have interefts detached from thofe of their conftituents, to act not only in direct violation of the truft repofed in them; but to the fentiments that many of them avowed out of parliament, when the nation furprifed by a fecond demand on its abufed generofity, was equally offended by the breach of faith, and at the juggle, by which the payment of the debts and an increafed eftablifhment, were artfully coupled together. I converfed at the time, with men of different parties in the Houfe of Commons, all of whom, either lamented that the fubject fhould have been brought forward, or they execrated the indecency of making fuch a requeft; while all of them entertained the fame opinion refpecting the conduct of his Royal Highnefs, and the principles from which *that* conduct has refulted:—They all agreed that *" the nation ought not to have heard of thofe debts, and, that it was not bound to pay them!"*

The former of thefe opinions was univerfal, and the difference that arofe on the latter, was more from motives of compaffion, than from a conviction that the Prince of Wales had a right to expect parliament to difcharge his debts—

From thefe opinions, fo univerfally acknowledged, and fo incontrovertibly true, it was reafonble to expect, that thofe who profeffed them, would have acted in conformity to their declaration, and refisted every attempt to engage parliament in a measure, from which disgrace to the Prince and dishonor to themselves, with perhaps much ultimate and serious mischief to the country, would ensue. But many of the men who held the language of truth out of parliament, contradicted their professions, and some of them their promises, by the vote they gave on the first instant, and connived at the delusion, by which the country, pressed and overwhelmed as it is with debt, is to be saddled with fresh burthens, in order to administer to the ruthless dissipation of a man, who has failed in the most essential of his engagements, and whose rank and affinity to the throne are opposed to the numberless well-founded charges that have been brought, not only against his discretion, but against his probity.

To this scandalous breach of faith to the nation—no answer was made;—no apology was offered! The silence observed upon the occasion, was a tacit acknowledgment of guilt, and they have left him to account for the FALSE-HOOD, with which he has abused the credulity of the nation.

To the reproach of indiscretion; to the unexaggerated charges of shameful and aggravated misconduct, nothing was opposed, but a pretended " *necessity for supporting the dignity of his illustrious rank, and the splendor of the* HEIR APPARENT," as if the accident of birth could (among beings calling themselves *rational*) atone for a deficiency of talents and of rectitude!

It was in vain that the few, who felt for the dignity of parliament; for the quiet of their country; for the wounded honor of the Prince; and above all, for the interests of a loyal and generous people, curbed to a premature impotence by the pressure of accumulating taxes, urged the indecency of transmitting his Royal Highness, branded to posterity on the journals of the House of Commons, as a LIAR! It was in vain that they beseeched parliament to PAUSE! and seriously contemplate the ruin that might ultimately ensue to the country and the Royal Family, by sanctioning the prodigality which impoverished the former, and dishonored the latter; their honest voice was stifled by the profligacy of their opponents, and the nation must unfortunately abide by the consequences! It is the duty of those who call themselves the friends of his Royal Highness, and who would deserve his confidence, to rescue him from a stigma so indelible. As an individual, interested in the preservation of the constitution, and anxious that the honor of all the branches of the Royal Family should be preserved unsullied, I cannot express in too strong language my apprehension, that much disrespect to the heir apparent, and much danger to the kingdom will ensue, if parliament should charge itself with the payment of debts, of which it ought not to take cognizance, and which by their interference, will be acknowledging in direct terms to the world, that the Prince of Wales, their probably future sovereign, is not fit to be trusted! Imprudent as he has acted, it would pain me to behold him fettered in private matters, which however they may import the moral character of the man, do not, and ought not, to fall within the jurisdiction of parliament. The line of conduct for the House of Commons to adopt, is very obvious, and cannot be mistaken, if its pride or purity should happily bear any affinity to the character that it *ought* to possess in the country.

It is in its power to rescue itself from the odium it inherits, from the known servility and disgraceful venality of *former* parliaments; the opportunity is certainly favourable; it is not yet too late, nor can it be too often repeated, or too vehemently urged, that the future quiet of the empire absolutely depends on the degree of fidelity, with which those who are deputed by the nation, to conduct its concerns, discharge the trust reposed in them.

They are unexpectedly, and in some measure, unfairly called upon, for a sum of money, their proportion of which, compared to that of their constituents, will be very small indeed, and this application for a portion of the public wealth, is made at a moment, when the country is in a ferment, and engaged in a war, the issue of which, is extremely doubtful, and which, if unfortunate, may lead to the greatest, and most dreadful of all calamities— a REVOLUTION! It is needless to dwell on the shameful indecency of such an application; those who are capable of making a fair estimate of the different pretensions of mankind to honors and rewards, will acknowledge, that it is nonsense or something worse, to plead the rank of the individual on this occasion, in justification of the demand, and by their decision I am content to abide—The object of this second Postscript is to warn Parliament, while it has yet the power to oppose its irrevocable fiat, of the alarm and despondency which their compliance will occasion throughout the British empire—I wish to forewarn Parliament of the dishonor it will entail on itself, and of the hazard to which it will expose the nation, by the recognition of debts, which it cannot descend to notice, consistent with its dignity and the justice that it owes to the country;—my intention is not to degrade, but to exalt Parliament in the public opinion: my object is to ensure it that respect, esteem, and veneration, to which it is entitled by the courtesy of the constitution, and to behold it, what it is supposed and ever ought, to be; the security of the people against fraud and oppression;—their refuge from despondency! I wish it to be considered and beloved as an efficient barrier, and our best safeguard against every species of encroachment on the part of the crown; as the only power to which it may be necessary to resort for protection or redress in the *last* instance, and the only power, by which regal licentiousness is to be curbed, or its delinquency punished. In a word, that the trust reposed in it may be executed with that firmness and integrity, which ought to characterise the senate of a free people, and which can alone ensure happiness and liberty to them and to their posterity. It is under the fullest conviction that the legal authority of Parliament is competent to all these important purposes, and that a confidence in its force, purity, and vigilance, can alone preserve its credit and stability, I assert it would have been wisdom, as well as justice in the House of Commons to have only noticed that part of the message from the throne, which related to an establishment for the Heir Apparent—It was the only line of conduct for the representatives of the people to have adopted, and the reproof to majesty would have been the stronger and more dignified by being SILENT! It is impossible but the King must have been apprised of the consequences that would result from an application to Parliament to discharge the debts of the Prince of Wales, after the assurance that had been given in 1787, that no such application would in future be made—The danger of such a measure must certainly have been suggested to his majesty—A silence on a matter so connected with his dignity and the quiet of the country, would have been criminal in the extreme, and I cannot think so ill of the confidential servants of the crown, and of the chancellor of the Exchequer in particular, as to believe them capable of so gross and unpardonable an omission—Mr. Pitt, pledged in some degree for the observance of the promise, (by having been the bearer of the former message) was more, than any other member of the Cabinet, called upon to state to his Royal Master, that the second message was no less injurious to his honor, than it was disrespectful to Parliament and the nation, and that being compelled by the situation he held to deliver the meffage, he could not obey his Majefty's commands without apprifing him of the mifchiefs that might refult from it.

That fuch a reprefentation was made cannot well be doubted—It would have been a breach of duty to the Sovereign, to the country and himfelf, not to have done it, and having done it, the Fiction in law which we have hitherto regarded, and cherifhed as a truth, is in a manner annihilated.

I will pafs over the indecency of embarraffing the perfons intrufted with the executive Government, with queftions of domeftic finance, with which the public have no concern; neither will I comment on the imprudence which reduced the Chancellor of the Exchequer to the painful alternative of either complying with a requifition unreafonable in point of fact, and certainly injudicious with refpect to time; or, of refigning, at the moft critical period of a war, the moft hazardous and moft important in which Great Britain was ever engaged. Thofe who are difpofed to cenfure the minifter for the election he has made, may not perhaps have fufficiently weighed in their own minds the very imminent rifque which would probably enfue from a change in his Majefty's councils, in the middle of a campaign, on the iffue of which the profperity and independance of the country depend? I do not propofe this queftion exclufively to thofe, who are of opinion that his Majefty failed in that refpect which he owes to his own character, when he failed in the promife which he gave to the nation in 1787, but to people of every rank and defcription, who have judgment to difcriminate, and candor to decide; of thefe I will afk, whether it would have been juftifiable in the Chancellor of the Exchequer, circumftanced as the country is at this aweful moment, to have expofed (which he would have done by his refignation) the arrangements he has made, his plans for offenfive and defenfive operations, the diftribution of the national force and refources, and the whole of his moft fecret meafures and engagements, to men (the probable fucceffors of himfelf and his colleagues) who have been in the conftant habit of oppofing every meafure of the crown, and who might from vanity, perfonal pique, and a variety of other motives, change, or neglect to profecute with vigor, meafures refolved upon, and refufe to ratify or execute engagements entered into with foreign princes? If there is rifk or impropriety in communicating the meafures of the cabinet to thofe who oppofe, and would perhaps gladly counteract them; that rifk, and that impropriety, would certainly become greater by invefting them with the power to cancel what they difapprove.

The part therefore which Mr. Pitt had to take, when Majefty had impofed upon him the ungracious tafk of communicating the meffage which has created fuch univerfal difguft and alarm, was obvious; he had no alternative but that of fubmiffion, or of endangering the fafety of the empire; and thus circumftanced, it was incumbent on the Houfe of Commons to have relieved him from the mortification of palliating, what cannot be defended, by referring his Majefty to his meffage in 1787, for an anfwer to that part of his meffage in 1795, which relates to the payment of the Prince of Wales's debts. Colonel Stanley, very much to his honor, pointed this out, on the very day that the queftion was agitated; he very properly called upon the clerk to read from the journals, the meffage which ought to have influenced their proceedings, and by which alone they ought to have been governed. Sir Geo. Shuckburgh *(a)*, Sir. Will. Young, Mr. H. Duncombe *(b)*, Mr. Grey, Mr.

(a) It is faid that a number of gentlemen, as independent in their minds,

Sturt, and a few others, took the same line as the gentleman who moved for a call of the house, and if some of those who professed similar principles, to the author of this pamphlet, had held the same manly language in parliament, that they held out of it, they would have a much better claim to the suffrages of their constituents at the next general election, than their conduct entitles them to at present; they would have saved by their consistency in some sort, the honor of the Prince and their own; they have brought both into question, and exposed parliament to suspicions incompatible with its credit and dignity. It is impossible that those gentlemen can have erred through ignorance; averse as I am to conferring the office of legislator on ideots, I would gladly avail myself of the plea of imbecillity to excuse a conduct, which I am afraid has lain the foundation of much future misery to the Prince, and of much serious mischief to the country; but to whatever motives this conduct may be attributed, I feel assured that not one of those, who admitted the question of the debts to be discussed, were aware of the numberless difficulties in which it would involve them; it did not occur to them perhaps, that by agreeing to pay those debts, either by a sum for the specific purpose, or by the juggle of an extravagant establishment, beyond the fair claim of any Prince of Wales, and certainly much more than the object in ques-

---

as they are known to be in their fortunes, assembled at Waghornes, to discuss the most effectual means of giving a decided negative to the question of debt. This meeting made up in character, what it wanted in numbers, and if the chairman, Mr. Powys, had shewn more firmness and decision, the country would have had infinite obligations to the association.

(b) The advice of this gentleman had much intrinsic value in it. There was eloquence, as well as truth in the good council he offered. "Retirement is indeed the nurse of reflection," and such a nurse as his Royal Highness will do well to consult, notwithstanding the advantages he may have derived from the good example, and wholesome admonitions of Mr. Sheridan.

tion deserves, that they would find themselves reduced to the necessity (in order to prevent the repetition of such applications) to come to some vote, or to frame some bill, on which the nation could better rely, than on the promise of his Majesty, or his son.

It did not occur to them perhaps, that by admitting a necessity in parliament to pay those debts, they declared his Royal Highness insolvent, while by reserving an annual sum for the payment of those debts, they virtually declared him unfit to manage his own concerns; the first measure is neither more nor less than a statute of bankruptcy; the second amounts to a statute of lunacy: and thus branded, marked, and stained by the legislature, the Heir Apparent to the British throne is dismissed, bound and fettered, not only as an infant, unfit to be trusted on the score of imbecility, but as a person who, having violated his word, is unworthy of confidence.

The House of Commons could not, consistently with their duty, have acted otherwise, after having taken upon themselves to make a provision for his debts, but they might have foreseen the dilemma in which such a measure would involve them, and have avoided it: they might have perceived the strong arguments it would furnish, not only to those who are disaffected to monarchy, but to those who think that the intellects of men ought to bear some proportion to the offices which they hold in society, and that their rectitude should be equal to the trust reposed in them. If these reflections had occurred to those gentlemen who were most active, and who pretend to be most attached to the Prince, I do not believe that they would have exposed him to the chance of having his succession disputed, or have given the numerous enemies of royalty, dispersed throughout the country, an opportunity of asking, with an insolent air of triumph, if a man convicted of a breach of promise, and so branded by parliament, is a proper object to succeed to the throne of his ancestors? Questions of this nature, and which unfortunately answer themselves, should be avoided. I really foresee much serious calamity to the country, if parliament should take upon themselves the payment of debts, which it was no less imprudent to have made a subject of discussion, than it was reprehensible to have contracted.

It is impossible for the representatives of the people to observe too much caution, or to be too careful that their measures do not afford a pretext to those whose vigilance is ever on the watch to degrade the legislature in the public mind, and deprive it of that confidence on which the peace, security, and stability of the government depend. Sedition derives less force from reason than from numbers; but when argument is added to the latter, its strength is invincible. Those who are entrusted with the administration of public affairs will do well to give this truth the attention it deserves. There is *security* in it. They will find it contains an antidote to the poison which has been disseminated throughout the country, and they will prevent by prudence, what they may find very difficult to suppress by violence. These are not times to play with the passions, or to irritate the minds of men: the question before parliament derives its importance more from the circumstances of the moment, and the mode and manner with which it has been brought forwards, than from its own intrinsic weight; strip it of these, and it will be divested of all that is offensive and dangerous. It is from this consideration that I wish the Commons of Great Britain to PAUSE! They are on a precipice, and they cannot be too circumspect. There is more mischief invelloped in a prompt decision than they suspect, and it is possible, that with every good wish towards his Royal Highnefs, and under the fulleft conviction that they are promoting his future intereft and comfort, they may lay the foundation for dethroning him, or for cutting off his fucceffion. They are not aware, perhaps, that by noticing his debts, they would neceffarily be compelled to fetter and reftrain his future expenditure, and that thefe reftrictions, juftified by his imprudence, would furnifh arguments in abundance to thofe whofe object is to fubvert the conftitution, and fubftitute in its ftead what they, either ignorantly or malicioufly, term a pure democracy.

The Commons are not aware perhaps that by taking upon themfelves to provide for the debts, they encourage in fome degree, the very turpitude and indifcretion which they reprobate; while by refufing to allow the Prince to difcharge his own incumbrances, they declare him in effect unworthy of all truft.

They are not aware that fuch a decifion (if it fhould unhappily take place) may hereafter be interpreted as a virtual difqualification, of which fome future faction may avail itfelf, and on the authority of parliament pronounce the Prince of Wales incapacitated for the office of fovereign; if men who are notorioufly averfe to our eftablifhments in church and ftate, fhould acquire fufficient force and credit to contend with the executive power, what anfwer can be given to them, if, taking the act of parliament, which they may poffibly call an act of exclufion, they fhould inquire, if a man under this accumulated odium, and difmiffed to the world with a character impeached, fullied, and in fome degree deftroyed by the legiflature, *is* a proper perfon to fucceed to the throne of Great Britain?

It is to be hoped that an event fo calamitous to himfelf and his country may never happen, and it is incumbent on parliament, called upon as it is, to guard againft the poffibility of it, and not to endanger, by a miftaken kindnefs, the rights of a man, whom it is at once their duty and their intereſt to preſerve from ruin and diſhonor.

Thoſe who hold a contrary doctrine, and who perceive no danger from a liberality as ill-timed as it is undeſerved, are very ill-qualified indeed to give an opinion on a ſubject ſo delicate and important, while thoſe who are for laviſhing the public treaſure to the very extent of the demands and expectations of his Royal Highneſs, are infinitely more hoſtile to the Heir Apparent and to parliament, and certainly much more to be dreaded, than the moſt virulent of thoſe who would baniſh the former, and ſupercede the authority of the latter.

I aver on the joint authorities of common ſenſe, and common honeſty, that the repreſentative dignity and integrity, ought not to be ſacrificed to the eaſe, ſplendor, or even comfort of any one family or individual whatever, and eſpecially of an individual, who has forfeited all claim to confidence or reſpect, by the public violation of his word, and ſtill more if poſſible by the little feeling he has ſhewn for the accumulated diſtreſſes of the people, whoſe blood and treaſures have been profuſly ſquandered in ſupporting his family on that throne, from which their predeceſſors were deſervedly driven for their exactions and tyranny— It never can paſs current, in any ſound and honeſt mind, that the ſecurity and felicity of millions are to be ſacrificed to the guilt and profuſion of one man, or that the intereſts of an entire nation are to be put in competition with the impudent pretenſions of incorrigible folly. If the Prince of Wales has involved himſelf in pecuniary difficulties, it is HIS duty to diſcharge them, and not that of the nation, who having allotted a very ample ſum for his income, has nothing to do with his debts—If the former allowance was inadequate, in the name of heaven let it be augmented to one hundred thouſand pounds—No objection will or can be made to the increase, but let it be his concern, to discharge his embarraſſments, and do not let Parliament degrade itſelf by becoming the aſſignees of a Royal Bankrupt—Let his Royal Highneſs go into retirement, as was recommended on Monday night, by an honeſt and independent member of the Houſe of Commons—The advice of Mr. H. Duncombe is ſalutary, and well worthy of conſideration;—it argues fidelity to his conſtituents, and reſpect for the Heir Apparent;—it breathes loyalty to the Throne, and affection to the country, and the Prince by adopting the council that has been offered, will recover the eſteem and confidence of the people with a much greater rapidity than he has loſt them.—In retirement he will derive advantages, by far more valuable and important than an emancipation from debt, and which from the univerſal change that has taken place in the minds of men, are become indiſpenſible. It is full time that Princes ſhould become ſenſible of their dependent and relative ſituation;—it is full time that they ſhould become competent to the duties of their profeſſion, and ceaſe to be tyrants or cyphers in their dominions.

The Bill on this important queſtion I am ſorry to find, is printed, and with a title which expreſsly declares, that *" Parliament will make a proviſion for the debts."* I was willing to attribute to an *error of the preſs,* what has a direct tendency to inſpire a well-founded diſtruſt of the integrity of the Houſe of Commons; I ſhould be ſorry to arraign the rectitude of that branch of the legiſlature to which I feel attached, and which, I call heaven to witneſs! it is my ſincereſt wiſh, ſhould preſerve its credit with the nation; but the duty that I owe to my country is paramount to all other conſiderations, and if the Houſe of Commons ſhould unfortunately betray the truſt repoſed in them; if they ſhould in ſervile complaiſance to the Heir Apparent, reſolve upon providing for debts, contracted in direct violation of a solemn promise; if they should, forgetful of their duty, become accomplices in the guilt that would defraud the country of SEVEN HUNDRED THOUSAND POUNDS, I hope that the other branch of the legiflature, the Peers of Britain! will have the virtue to come forward and interpofing their authority, stand (as they have done) between a corrupt and dangerous influence, and rescue at once their country from ruin, and its legiflature from ignominy.

This is the hope of every honest and well-difpofed subject in the kingdom; it is the wish of every friend to order and good government; of those who, detefting anarchy, wish to avoid the neceffity of an APPEAL, the confequences of which it is impoffible to forefee, and which the Commons of Great Britain have it in their power to avoid by a pofitive and peremptory refufal to provide for the payment of debts contracted by vice and folly, and which AVARICE combined with DESPOTISM would infolently and unfeelingly extort from a generous and impoverished people.

THIRD POSTSCRIPT.

IT has been insinuated, with a degree of industry proportioned to the malignancy of the falsehood, that the foregoing pages have received the countenance of his Majesty's Ministers:—The respect which is due to the confidential servants of the crown, independent of that strict and inflexible attachment to truth, from which no consideration shall ever seduce or compel me to depart, requires that I should give a direct and immediate contradiction to a calumny, as atrocious in design, as it is impudent in assertion. I have not the slightest communication with any member of the cabinet, nor will I ever consent, whatever my good wishes towards administration may be, to square my principles by their convenience. The profusion of the male branches of the Royal Family, and their contempt of all decency, are matters of public notoriety; their levity has been the constant topic of conversation and complaint in all societies; every voice has been raised against them, and all ranks and descriptions of people have expressed their alarms at an obstinacy bordering upon insanity, which bidding defiance to all admonition, might be productive of much serious mischief to the country. The constitution has been brought into hazard, by the strong arguments which their conduct furnish against royalty, and this danger has been increased by an application to Parliament in a moment of extreme calamity and diftrefs, for pecuniary aid to difcharge debts moft idly and moft fhamefully contracted, after a folemn promife had been given to the nation, that the people fhould not be called upon, a SECOND TIME.

The fanctity of the engagement has been violated, and I have cenfured the violation with the feverity it deferves, but not with the feverity which I could have done, from the facts in my poffeffion. If there is any thing criminal in what I have written, the guilt is entirely my own— minifters are perfectly innocent; they were neither acceffaries before, nor after the fact, and I believe that the Letter to the Prince, is in as little favor at the Treafury, as it is at Carleton Houfe. As to the opinion of the *noble* Lord, who recommended a profecution to be inftituted againft the author, it is merely the opinion of an individual, who has been floated by the turbulence of paft times, and the natural turbulence of his own temper, from poverty and obfcurity, into credit and affluence, and as fuch deferves neither credit nor attention;—it is merely the refult of a mind difeafed; of a mind as coarfe and overbearing, as it is known to be wayward, petulant, reftlefs, and diffatisfied; of a mind in love with power and impatient of controul;—perpetually cavilling, grumbling, and finding fault with every body and every thing, without inclination or capacity to amend what it condemns, or magnanimity to pardon what offends or contradicts it; proving by its very defpotifm its complete difqualification for what it moft defires, and rendering it the common intereft of all, that it fhould be impotent and null. This captious Peer, hacknied in wrong, and better verfed in legal fubtleties, than in the principles of legiflation, has in fome degree authorifed the flanders which he affected to difcountenance, by requiring miniftry (as a proof of their innocence) to profecute the author of this letter as a *libeller:* this advice, to fay nothing worfe of it, is fufpicious; nor does it redound to the honor of his Lordfhip's underftanding, that he fhould have councilled government to commit its dignity, and hazard fomething more than its credit, by a conteft with reafon, fupported by facts—I think, if he had confulted, either his library, or his experience, that he would have been lefs precipitate, and that if his memory had not failed him, the recollection of his hiftory and good fortune would have taught him, humility and filence;—I defire no other Weapon to fell this Coloffus, than his Character—A variety of other reports have been circulated, (with a view to check the influence, and retard the progrefs of truth,) which it does not become me to notice—It would be an endlefs tafk indeed, to refute every idle rumor, that goffipping ignorance or mifchievous malice may fabricate. I have little leifure for fuch occupation, and the noble Lord may venture to believe me when I affure him, that I have as little relifh for *Canterbury* tales as his Lordfhip, though not precifely from the *fame* motive—That he is a better judge of what conftitutes a libel, and that he has gained more by profecuting fuch publications, than the author of the preceding pages, ever wifhes to gain by writing them, will readily be admitted by thofe, who are acquainted with the characters of the two men, but that a love of litigation, fhould in the very decline of life, triumph over the mild dictates of policy and equity, is a melancholy proof of the wonderful force and influence of habit! That this man fo much indebted to accident, and fo little to merit for his extraordinary fuccefs in life, fhould wifh to involve the Prince in a conteft where " *much may be loft, and nothing can be gained*".—neither argues difcretion nor affection, for affection would have given better council, and at his age, we expect the judgment to be more temperate and correct—but his Lordship, I am afraid is too old to learn morality, or I could school him to better purposes!—If however his advice should be adopted, and the bookseller be required by legal process to discover the author of the offensive Letter, my name will be no longer a secret; I shall feel myself bound in honor to come forward, and shield, if possible, an innocent man, dependent on his industry for a maintenance, from the consequences which may ensue, and for which I ought to be responsible. It is impossible to say at present, what interpretation the laws may give to my well-intentioned zeal; but whenever they are called upon to decide, my attachment to the constitution will be acknowledged, even by those who have been the most active in arraigning it; the justice of the cause I have espoused, inspires me with confidence, and I am prepared for the event. The mind, conscious of its rectitude, cannot sink into despondency; its strength and exertions will ever keep pace with occasion, and I will cheerfully trust my fortune, my liberty, and my reputation, to the verdict of an ENGLISH JURY.

Shortly will be published, by J. OWEN, *Piccadilly*,

AN ADDRESS TO THE BISHOPS,

ON THE

DANGER TO BE APPREHENDED

TO OUR

ECCLESIASTICAL ESTABLISHMENTS

FROM THE

CONDUCT AND BAD EXAMPLE

OF SOME OF THE

NON-RESIDENT PAROCHIAL CLERGY.

Where may be had, Price 14s

TRAVELS THROUGH SWITZERLAND, ITALY, SICILY, THE GREEK ISLANDS, TO CONSTANTINOPLE, &c. &c.

By THOMAS WATKINS, A. M. F. R. S.

www.ingramcontent.com/pod-product-compliance
Lightning Source LLC
Chambersburg PA
CBHW031403160426
43196CB00007B/875